About The Cover

Photos:

1. Large photo James Dolmage with a 'run up the strong man and land on your feet kick' to Steve Dietz in 1978. Grant Kirby photo

Left to Right small photos

2. James delivering karate ridgehand to Anthony Septinelli. Grant Kirby
3. James with wrestling double leg takedown to Anthony. Grant Kirby
4. James at 5'8" delivering TKD roundhouse kick to 6'5" Anthony. Grant Kirby
5. Bethany 'Sparky' Wallace. Dolmage
6. Bobbie 'Bo-San' McGrath delivering flying sidekick to James. Tony Hostetter
7. "Sparky" with jujitsu rear naked choke to U.S. Naval Special Ops member Tyler Wallace. Dolmage
8. James with Hapkido wrist attack to Aaron 'Thor' Maddron.

Book layout and design by James Dolmage. Technological assistance provided by 'Dr.' Greg Fernandez.

All rights reserved. No part of this publication may be reproduced or transmitted in any form or by any means, electronic, mechanical, including photocopy, recording, or any information storage and retrieval system, without permission in writing from the publisher.

Copyright © 2017 by James W. Dolmage email jdbudo@msn.com

Table of Contents

1. TO START
    ABOUT THE COVER.. 1
    TABLE OF CONTENTS... 2
    PREFACE.. 4
    DEFINITION OF MODERN MARTIAL ARTS............... 7
    MODERN MARTIAL ARTS CHART............................. 8
    JD'S MARTIAL HISTORY.. 9

2. REGULAR CHAPTERS
    OPTIMUM WEIGHT... 14
    SELF DEFENSE VS MMA.. 21
    STRENGTH TRAINING... 26
    BALANCE.. 44
    BASICS.. 49
    KICKS.. 56
    EVOLUTION OF MMA... 61
    STRIKING WITH TECHNIQUE.................................... 69
    AGING... 77
    BREATHE.. 81
    NATURAL BEHAVIOR... 86
    FLUID MOTION... 89
    SPIRIT STRENGTH... 92
    LEAD WITH BOTH SIDES.. 96
    VALUES... 101
    FORMS.. 105

3. SOME IMPORTANT MEN
    JI BIOGRAPHY.. 113
    ED PARKER... 115

4. BORROWED WISDOM
    JAPANESE TERMS... 117
    FOOD FOR THOUGHT.. 119
    APACHE.. 121
    PREPARATION OF A WARRIOR................................ 123

GENGHIS KAHN	124
JET RULES	126
UFAF	129
WHAT IT TAKES	131
WINNERS	133
DESIDERATA	134

5. WEAPONS CHAPTERS

WEAPON BASICS	135
FIREARM SAFETY	139
FIREARM TERMS	143
MINDSET	154
AMMUNITION	161
SHOTGUNS	167
RIFLES	171
ATOMIC BULLET	174

6. FINISH UP

ACKNOWLEDGMENTS	176
FINAL THOUGHTS	177

7. REVISED CHAPTERS

WHAT IS NEW..	178
NEWER FIGHTERS...	181
PENETRATION TEST...	187
NEW WORLD RECORD..	189

Preface

To begin this book, I would like to make it clear that I consider myself first and foremost a good student of the MARTIAL ARTS. A "martial arts guy" as Hapkido Grandmaster Ji, Han Jae says. I have no illusion that I know everything about fighting.

I have learned a considerable amount of information over the past 5 decades, and many people I meet don't know some of the things I have learned, so it's time to share some interesting, inspirational and useful things. I have not created this Warrior Training book to be like other books. It looks different and the content isn't traditional in format or appearance.

I don't want to be the same; I enjoy change and different things the Martial Arts have to offer. I hope you open your mind, as Ed Parker said, "Your mind is like a parachute, it only works when it's open". Please sample my cup of tea. There is much ahead for both of us to learn.

Empty your cup before you taste my cup of tea.

"The emptiness of the cup is it's usefulness"

I try to learn from anyone who seems to have something useful to offer, maybe even you but now I am more selective of who I listen to. I have learned that some things taught are not really practical for me but those philosophies and techniques may be useful for you. This book is meant to give ideas and is "nothing special" as Bruce Lees said about his art. There is a great deal of knowledge, skills and information that you may not have yet but that knowledge is out there; it just takes time and experience to learn and implement.

It's my desire to instill into others the proper values ingrained into me by my coaches and instructors who have shared their knowledge with me. After 51 years I continue seek useful knowledge and so should you. A real martial artist understands that their arts should be practiced for their lifetime. Principles of honesty, respect for yourself and others, courtesy, hard work ethics, persistence and a general 'can do' attitude are a large part of martial arts training. I hope you absorb this as a central theme of my work here.

Some information presented here to you may not agree with what your instructor says and you may not be ready to understand some of it. All the material in this book is what respected, wise, tough men and women who have excelled in some aspect of martial arts or combat, have shared with me. It's NOT my knowledge, it's from them and most have inflicted some pain on me before I considered what they had was worth learning.

Some very useful information has been gathered by reading, one can always learn something that way but it's not the same to learn physical techniques form a book or magazine. You must put in the hours to physically train. There is no substitute for your hard work and experience. This book is less about how to execute individual physical techniques (that will

James is kicking 3 weeks before his 63rd birthday wearing his G.P.H.S. wrestling shirt from his senior year at high school in 1972. He weighs the same here as he did at the beginning of the wrestling season 45 years ago. Thanks to Dr. Scot Thorsen for his trust.

come in later work) and more about educating your brain (your best weapon) to many things a well rounded martial artist or person interested in protecting themselves, needs to know. It's more for your ***mind and spirit.***

I have included some information I didn't write but felt other martial artists will also find it interesting and beneficial. I want to respect intellectual property and give credit where it is due. In some cases such as the Genghis Khan story, I could have simply rewritten some of the information but that's not respecting the author. Some information I have kept for decades and have no idea of it's origin. When I first began saving information or pictures I found interesting, there was no thought of putting it into a book. I just liked what I saw and saved it. Now I wish I would have been more detailed so I could let others know the source.

I want to give thanks and credit to the sources of photos. Many photos of Muhammad Ali were taken by Neil Leifer and Howard Bingham but years ago I cut photos out of books so I could put them up and look at and now I don't know who to give credit to. If I try to guess the photos source and am wrong, that won't be good. If you want more great and inspirational photos of Ali, contact those men.

There are many photos from the Ring Magazine, KO magazine, Boxing Illustrated, as well as Black Belt magazine, Karate Illustrated, Inside Kung Fu and other magazines, newspapers and books. If you are seeking martial arts knowledge, buy these magazines and learn. There are many other new martial arts publications offered today.

Thank you for wanting to learn Modern Martial Arts. I hope your journey is safe, healthy, and fun. While the subject is serious I like to have fun. If you don't have fun you won't stick around to practice, so if there is something in this book you think is goofy, it just may be I'm having some fun! ;-)

Respectfully,
James Dolmage
(friends call me JD so you will see those initials throughout this book)

Definition of *Modern* MARTIAL ARTS

Definition of MODERN

1. **a** : of, relating to, or characteristic of the present or the immediate past : CONTEMPORARY <the *modern* American family>

    b : of, relating to, or characteristic of a period extending from a relevant remote past to the present time <*modern* history>

2. : involving recent techniques, methods, or ideas : UP-TO-DATE <*modern* methods of communication>

3. *capitalized* : of, relating to, or having the characteristics of the present or most recent period of development of a language <*Modern* English>

Definition of MARTIAL

1. : of, relating to, or suited for war or a warrior <*martial* music> <a *martial* tone of voice — Tim Appelo> <*martial* prowess>

2. : relating to an army or to military life <*martial* discipline> <stories of *martial* tradition — Ewen Macaskill>

3. : experienced in or inclined to war : WARLIKE <its *martial* people fought the British to a standstill — Mary Anne Weaver>

   —**martially** \-shə-lē\ *adverb*

Definition of ART

1. : skill acquired by experience, study, or observation <the *art* of making friends>

2. **a** : a branch of learning: (1) : one of the humanities (2) **arts** *plural* : LIBERAL ARTS

    b *archaic* : LEARNING, SCHOLARSHIP

3. : an occupation requiring knowledge or skill <the *art* of organ building>

4. **a** : the conscious use of skill and creative imagination especially in the production of aesthetic objects <the *art* of painting landscapes>; *also* : works so produced <a gallery for modern *art*>

    b (1) : FINE ARTS (2) : one of the fine arts (3) : one of the graphic arts

> Modern Martial Arts is not a style of martial arts, it's simply the open minded study of martial arts in general, regardless of nationality, culture, or prejudice. It considers there are many different reasons and goals for the study of martial arts, ranging from strictly health and fitness, to mental and spiritual improvements, self protection, fighting competitions, or combat military work.

Modern Martial Arts

Traditional Values – Modern Approach
Training and Teaching since 1965

Fitness
You may never need self-defense, but you need health and fitness everyday

Conditioning	Shadow box/kickboxing
Coordination	Partner box/kickbox pad work
Strength	Non-contact sparring drills
Flexibility	Bag circuit training
Balance	Sports medicine/science

Self-Defense
If you ever need to protect yourself or those you love, you will be grateful

Defense Tactics	Kenpo
Hapkido	Weapons

Sport Competitions
For serious students wanting to challenge themselves outside their school

Full Contact MMA	Boxing	Karate
Wrestling	JuJitsu	Kickboxing
	Judo	

Mental / Spiritual Development
Martial Arts teaches Character

Positive Attitudes	Discipline
Respect	Perseverance
Courtesy	Hard work ethics

MARTIAL ARTS BACKGROUND

James Dolmage, 24 months, with toy handguns.

Before I was 2 years old it seemed I loved to have a toy handgun in my hand. Many photos taken of me when I was a kid include a safe toy weapon of some type.

It seemed natural to me then and continues to seem so. Any weapon including firearms, is simply an extension of your hands.

JD, 22 months, with a handgun in one hand and a guard dog in the other.

My formal unarmed fighting arts training began in 1965 at age 11 in the Kid Wrestling program headed by National Wrestling Hall of Fame coach 'Wild Bill' Ryder, who was inducted as a high school coach. I wrestled competitively through Jr. and Sr. High school and in some college 'open' wrestling tournaments.

I believe wrestling is the fundamental martial art. Anyone who really wants to be an effective all around martial artist needs to get on the mat with the wrestlers. From there all the other arts can be absorbed usefully according to the practitioners capabilities and desires. Boxing was next in 1968 under George Eckstein. He worked briefly with George Foreman who was a member of the

Grants Pass Job Corps before becoming the 1968 Olympic Gold Medalist and Heavyweight Champion of the World.

In 1967 I began buying Black Belt Magazine. September's issue had Joe Lewis on the cover. Years later when I asked Mr. Lewis to autograph it, he told me that he was the first tournament fighter to be on the cover of Black Belt magazine. Until that time only instructors had been featured on the cover.

The next month Bruce Lee was on the cover as Kato. Even back then Bruce was writing about the advantages of keeping an open mind and exploring different styles. He was an original

mixed martial artist.

I started tae kwon do training in 1969, jujitsu in 1971 and judo in 1973. The chokes, joint locks, throws, rolls and break-falls from these arts were perfect supplements to the deficiencies that wrestling had for street defense. Kicking from TKD (tae kwon do) gave me more range and power than boxing punches gave me but seemed dangerous in some environments. Boxing foot work, punch defense and punching power seemed more effective than the TKD punching method but I thought getting kicked in the face was extremely impressive.

By the mid 1970s I had learned enough from vastly different arts to wonder how these fighting arts could be so different in philosophy and approach. They had such different answers to the same situation or technique I was learning to defend against. I continued to learn about interesting and different approaches from various styles of karate as well.

David Massender trusts JD   Grant Kirby

In 1977 I met Mr. Herb Steet, who at the time had trained for 14 years under Ed Parker. Mr. Steet had also trained under Mike Stone, Chuck Norris, Dan Inosonto, Tak Kubota, Dave Hebler and others. He took me to fight in my first International Karate Championship in Long Beach, CA in 1978. The first person to defeat me in karate competition was Manuel Urquidez.

Mr. Herb Steet

By the time I met Mr. Steet, I was training, learning and teaching martial arts full time. I competed for 23 years in distance running races, boxing, wrestling, black belt karate, black belt judo and USPSA handgun shooting competitions. My goal was to compete with others at their 'game,' knowing I would be at a disadvantage to those who concentrated on their favorite sport but I really wanted to understand different methods.

Working out with others is good but getting in the ring, on the mat or on the shooting line in front of others in actual competition is a

Ji, Han Jae in Golden Belt with Bruce Lee in Lee's final movie **Game of Death**

L to R 10th dan Grandmaster Ji, 8th dan Master Freda, and JD in Chicago for Scott Kifer's Hapkido seminar in 1990.

much more effective teacher. Most folks don't want to get their butts kicked, especially with everyone watching. That takes courage. I also believe a real warrior should be able to run 10 miles then fight. The Apaches would sometimes cover 40 miles on foot at night and then surprise their enemies first thing in the morning. They were tough people.

In the late 1980s I had the good fortune to have Grand Master Ji, Han Jae walk into the martial arts school I was managing in the San Francisco Bay area. Grand Master Ji is the founder of Hapkido and had fought with Bruce Lee in his final movie **GAME OF DEATH**. In this movie Bruce had Ji wear a golden belt to represent the **"Highest Level"** of martial artist. Which was Bruce Lee's opinion of Ji.

Ji had been in charge of instructing the South Korean Presidential bodyguards, police, military, and Special Forces. In addition, he had participated in a United States Pentagon information exchange program teaching U.S. Secret Service, F.B.I. and Office of Special Investigation personnel.

I arranged and assisted Grand Master Ji with seminars across the U.S. from California to New York. He was always a source of interesting philosophies, techniques and ideas with more *real martial arts* experience than anyone I have learned about. He taught me a tremendous amount of new and interesting information. For a time I lived above his San Francisco dojang ate many meals at his home and, in 1992 published his real story in the premier edition of Inside Tae Kwon Do magazine.

Ji opened my eyes to many things and I will always be grateful and honored to have shared so much time with such a Great Man. Among the many memories I have of him, is a time he was talking about real martial arts with me. He mentioned that if one competes in sport fight competitions and are scored on, one may lose a match. Then his tone changed. **"You make mistake in real martial arts YOU DIE!"** He lost his job of 18 years protecting the President of South Korea when assassins armed with M16's shot and killed President Park and many of Ji's fellow bodyguards while he was off duty.

(L) to (R) Shelly aka CB, brother Matt, JD, Bill, Allan in 1978 at Ed Parker's International Karate Championships. Scruffy bunch, huh? Manual Urquidez was 1st person to beat JD, 5-4 in Karate Fighting competition, light weight black belt division.
Herb Steet

It's impossible to give much of a detailed history of a lifetime of learning and practicing in a few pages. My goal has been to seek out and learn from the very best and find out what they did that was different from the others. I wanted to know how Champions thought, trained and fought. What did they eat? Who trained them? Which things worked for them and why? Knowledge is power and the more I learned the more interesting my quest for knowledge and ability seemed to be.

Some of the people I personally sought out included Ali, Frazier, Foreman, Leonard, Lewis, Norris, Urquidez, Couture, Ed Parker plus many, many others from sport fights. Others, such as Ji or Army Brigadier General Bushong, had their experiences in military or police weapon fighting. All were respected by those who know about fighting.

My goal now is to share my learning efforts with those who have an interest, and desire to know the MARTIAL WAY.

1969 **six months before Woodstock.** JD back row 2nd from the left, was 9th grade Distict Wrestling Champion of Southern OR.

The Daily Courier

10 years later in 1979, 5'8" JD right foot spin kicks at 6'5" Anthony Septinelli. Grant Kirby

2009, **40 years after JD's first wrestling championship**, right foot spin kicks at 6'7" Devin Tandy.

2009, JD left foot spin kicks to 'The Destroyer.' **Very Few old wrestlers in the world are able to do this,** which makes knee, leg, or groin kicks very simple and accurate.

VARSITY WRESTLING TEAM: Row 1: J.Dolmage, M.Wooldridge, B.Slack, S.Bottorff, R.Shipley, G.Taylor, D.Dean, R.Rietmann. Row 2: R. ely, T.McMahan, P.Simonsen, S.Boyer, K.Fuller, P.Doorly, D.Woodruff, P.Randall, R.Anderson. Row 3: K.Troyer, J.McLain, J.Mason, P.Stoner, Loss, C.Hough, J.Myers, J.Barnett, J.Weaver, K.McLean. Row 4: D.Robinson, J.Zering, J.Dietrich, M.Allison, D.Cook, D.Richards, R.Flickinger, bblitt, B.McMahon.

JD center with Capitol wrestling shirt. In 1972 Grants Pass high school qualified 12 of 26 wrestlers or **46%** (1 missing in photo) from the Southern Oregon Conference District Championships, for the State Championships held in Corvallis, OR. Randy Couture later wrestled and coached there at OSU. While this is certainly not as impressive as NCAA Division 1 wrestling, JD chose to kick, punch and apply submissions better than those whose focus was on wrestling.

OPTIMUM WEIGHT

JD in his younger days. Many years of hard work and proper diet will make you feel great. Having a fit and flexible body is a wonderful feeling money can't buy. Show up ready for competition, or just enjoy life because you are healthy and fit.   Grant Kirby

Many competitors must get on a scale and 'make weight' to compete in a contest or fight. Sometimes making weight is tougher than the fight itself.

Sometimes a fighter attempting to make the weight limit undergoes some very severe stresses on his body and some are not healthy. There are right and wrong ways to make the weight limit and some wrestlers have died trying.

I remember watching the heavyweight wrestlers in Jr. and Sr. High School. They usually enjoyed the great luxury of eating what they wanted. Even watching them drink water made those of us struggling to make weight very envious. Those Bastards!

Until you have undergone that type of sacrifice or you are lost in the desert, it's hard to imagine why a cup of water is such a precious thing. Many people with no interest in fitness, conditioning and competition, don't even enjoy water; it's too boring. They drink soda or other sweetened drinks instead which contributes a great deal to excess fat. Moderation is the key. Even something as essential and vital to life as breathing oxygen can be over done causing you to hyperventilate and pass out.

As a heavyweight, Evander Holyfield always entered the ring as a Warrior. He paid the price in training. I never saw him in less than magnificent physical condition. A young Muhammad Ali, Ken Norton Sr, Roy Jones Jr, Ken Shamrock, or Georges St. Pierre, and Randy Couture are among other fighters who always showed up lean and ready to fight. These men 'paid the price,' and in their daily lives thought, ate, drank and breathed World Championship.

Everything they ingested into their body had a purpose; to make or keep them The Champion.

Champions from fighting competitions will tell you that being the Worlds Best meant they had to sacrifice more than the others. Being the Champ meant when the others went out to party and do what most people were doing, they usually didn't. They had a focus, a dream, a burning desire to be the best at whatever form of competition it was.

It's my belief that Chuck 'The Iceman' Liddell shortened his reign as UFC Lt. Heavyweight Champion because of his fondness for partying. YouTube has an example of his apparent behavior. (search 'Chuck Liddell wasted.') I really enjoyed watching Mr. Liddell fight and am sorry that he had too much fun. He suffered the consequences.

A young JD in a kenpo stance.
Grant Kirby

If you are lucky enough to reach the top don't listen to and believe everyone who tells you how great you are. Remember you are the target for all those hungry fighters who are after your Title. The serious ones aren't out partying. They are coming for you!

A hungry young fighter with a poor upbringing usually has an advantage from a fighter's point of view. They couldn't get soft from the nicer things in life. Carlos Monzon grew up in the slums of Argentina. I read that four of Joe Frazier's siblings died of malnutrition in a South Carolina swampland. Roberto Duran came from poverty on the streets in Panama. As a lightweight and welterweight his fury, savagery and blistering pace was largely due to his upbringing as a poor kid surviving on the streets.

Duran owns the boxing record for most years between his first and last World Championship fights at 26 years, 4 months. That's a long time fighting, especially at that level. I have tremendous respect and admiration for those who make it to the top, living such a Spartan and hard fighter life.

I have even more admiration for those like Holyfield, De La Hoya or Roy Jones Jr because they have continued to show up in magnificent, top fighting condition even as multimillionaires who certainly don't *have* to get up at zero-dark-

Ali in his early 20s with a photo caption reading, **"I'll take my money and run."** He was addressing those who didn't like his style of mobile hit and run tactics.

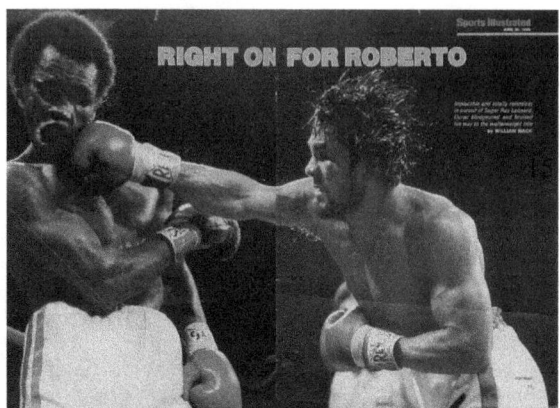

Duran got into Leonard's head, before this 1st fight, with many personal insults. Ray wanted to show him who's boss and rough him up at his own game instead of using his mobility and classic boxing skills. Ray was defeated but used smarter tactics for a win in the rematch.

Sports Illustrated

Fitz is an inspirational young lady kick boxer who likes to fight. She runs a kickbox facility in Florida and teaches those who want to get into or stay in shape. Check her out! Joseph Barbribe
FITZNESS.COM

thirty and run and go to the gym and take a daily beating.

These men work so hard most people on the planet Earth would die trying to do *one* of their day's activities, not even counting the sparring abuse. They can pay people to do most anything but they can't get by without doing the necessary training. They must pay the price *themselves* with sweat and blood.

In 1980, in the tunnel on the way to the locker room following 'Sugar' Ray Leonard's loss to Roberto Duran in their first fight, Ray noticed his team acting dejected. He asked them, "Why is everyone so sad? We just made $10,000,000!" That's 30 years ago when $10 Million bought much more than it does now! Elite boxers work unbelievably hard and earn the multimillions of dollars they are paid.

At the opposite end is James 'Lights Out' Toney who showed up fat and nowhere near good condition, to fight 47-year old stud Randy Couture in UCF 118. Toney had hard work ethics and discipline when he fought at 160 – 175 lbs. In a much anticipated fight between a former multi-division World Champion boxer, and a world class wrestler, MMA fighter, Toney disappointed many by lazily waddling in for his MMA debut fight at 237 lbs.

I expected James Toney to respect the UFC and fans by showing up ready to fight. He let us down but I know he got paid anyway and he didn't care what we thought.

If you have never traveled to a competition spitting in a cup, trying to shed that last half-pound, you wouldn't understand. Your optimum weight is not just about being dried out and starved but it

JD and sister-in-law, Shelly aka 'CB' for Cup Buster. Nickname earned by kicking a male in the groin and breaking his protective cup.

represents the weight you are most efficient at. It's an optimum condition where your speed, endurance, reflexes and strength have all come together. A higher weight may mean you have more raw strength, but your quickness is negatively affected. It also means your endurance will be reduced because you are packing excess baggage and your reflexes will slow.

When you are underweight, you feel light and quick but you will soon feel much weaker when pushed hard. You have even less endurance than when you are a bit heavy and your strength suffers a lot. On a few occasions, with over 23 years of mixed competitive fighting experiences, I lacked discipline and waited too long to drop weight. I tried taking the easy way out by starving off some pounds and drying out close to fight time. I made weight and promptly ran out of gas when the fight started.

It's much better to get down close to your weight limit a week or at least some days before your fight and hover close to the weight you need to be. If you are lucky enough to weigh in the day before you compete, and have time to re-hydrate and eat a couple of good meals before competition, you can gain 10 pounds. If you began dropping soon enough, trained and ate properly and are at your optimum weight, you should feel like a million bucks. Competing the same day within a couple of hours of getting on the scale and making the limit is a totally different story than competing the next day.

National Wrestling Hall of Fame coach 'Wild Bill' Ryder had a very good rule for his high school wrestling team. We were required to weigh in Monday afternoon within 4 pounds of the weight we wanted to wrestle that week. If we wrestled on Thursday night or Saturday for a tournament, we had at least 4 days to get the remaining 4 or so pounds off for the competition. Weighing more than 4 pounds over your weight limit close to competition makes it tough to lose without negatively effecting a wrestlers performance. Some may scoff at 4 pounds to lose but if you are already a lean, mean fighting machine, it's nowhere near as easy to lose properly as it is for a chubby fella. We also had to compete within a few hours of making weight, not the next day. As already stated, there's a huge difference.

Being dehydrated while competing doesn't work and can be dangerous. Everyone is different as far as how long it takes to recuperate and properly re-hydrate. Sometimes recuperation takes less time for someone who cuts weight frequently and is accustomed to it. Other times the person accustomed to 'the cut' may push it one too many times and their body may just decide it's had enough of that.

Your body is about 70% water and needs enough fluids to allow your nervous system to function properly. If not, you flat run out of gas and get whipped unless you compete against a 'fish' (wimp). If you try to re-hydrate too close to competing, you run the risk of having too much water in your stomach or having a full bladder in the midst of competition.

JD in 1969 as 9th grade District Wrestling Champion at 157 lbs. Two years later, JD lost in the District Finals 21 lbs less, at his optimum weight of 136 lbs. The guys JD defeated earlier at 157 were beaten with hustle, conditioning and desire and not the best wrestling technique ever seen.
The Daily Courier

You are the best judge of your optimum weight. Having an experienced coach who knows you and your performance over time helps. Only you know how you feel. Knowing how to 'peak' for a tournament so you are not over or under trained is important if you are a competitive fighter. Having the guidance of someone who has been there and helped others to do the same is extremely helpful to your conditioning education. Your personal experiences and education help you to determine your best weight.

Being at your optimum weight even as a heavyweight with no weight limitations will only help you perform your best. Bruce Lee had an adult weight that varied from 145 to around 126 lbs around the time he died. There are photos of him in a pose similar to a body builder pose when he was 'heavy.' His friends mentioned their concern at his weight loss and lack of rest near the time of his death.

As your body matures and grows, your optimum weight changes. Thomas 'The Hit Man' Hearns is a good example. At 6'1" and 147 lbs fighting 'Sugar Ray' Leonard, the 'Hit Man' looked very thin. At 160 lbs, fighting

Sucking Canal Sand
1971 JD wrestling in the District Finals at 136 lbs with torn knee cartilage on both sides of his right knee. Ryder's wrestlers were taught to go until your lungs felt like they were sucking canal sand, so that's what's happening here. If the only way you could hurt your opponent legally within the rules was to not quit and pressure them that's what we did. Nathan Conkle is hurting here only because JD went hard and didn't quit.

'Marvelous' Marvin Hagler for the Title, the 'Hit Man' still looked too thin. His skinny legs couldn't keep him mobile in one of the most exciting, action packed 8 minutes in all boxing history. In the post fight interview, Hearns said he was tired after the blistering pace of the first round. If you are a fight fan (if you are reading this you probably are) and have never seen the Hagler – Hearns fight, watch it on YouTube. It's exciting! I believe Hearns was simply fighting at too low a weight for his body. The Hagler fight was a MULTIMILLION-DOLLAR fight for Hearns, he had his pride and wanted to prove himself.

Hearns was last fighting in 1999 at the 190 lb cruiser-weight limit. He allowed himself to eat, his body filled out and he was stronger. That's 43 lbs and 6 weight divisions heavier than when he and 'Sugar' Ray Leonard battled it out in the early 1980s.

There are so many diet books on the market and some of them could easily confuse, mislead and negatively affect you. If you aren't a competitive fighter but you want to lose some fat and unwanted pounds to improve yourself and your physical condition remember; **DIETS *DON'T WORK* FOR LONG TERM WEIGHT LOSS.** Losing weight is not the correct mental approach. Since muscle weighs more than fat, with hard work and proper diet, some people can gain weight but lose fat and look, feel and perform far better than before. Don't think of losing weight. **Lose fat.**

Losing fat is theoretically very simple. To lose unwanted fat properly, there are only two things necessary: Only put good food and drink in your body and less of it. Burn more calories than you consume. You knew that! For some reason, some people just don't get that. I get tired of hearing the percentages of Americans who are overweight or obese! OK, I said it, lets move along.

Many people don't know which foods are good for them. I see people buy snacks because it says '0 fat' grams. They ask me if I want some, and I say "No thank you." They tell me, "It's OK, it has no fat!" I have them look at the label, and the first 3 or 4 ingredients are sugar related. Most of the rest of the ingredients are artificial flavors or chemicals. As 'Wild Bill' Ryder used to say, "It's crap." Read labels and educate yourself before you put it in your mouth. Ask yourself if what you are eating or drinking will help make you lean or be a champion.

Two very good sources of information to help you with what you eat are the books **Nutripoints** by Dr. Roy E. Vartabedian, and **Fit or Fat** by Covert Bailey. Mr. Bailey is an expert in the biochemistry of how your body utilizes the food you eat but most important he can convey his knowledge to the non-expert in interesting, nontechnical language. Even I can understand it! I kept his book on my table for 6 months, opening it up at random and reading whatever was there. I read that book again and again while I was eating.

Nutripoints is the most efficient, effective way I know of to find out which foods are good and which are not good for you. Using modern computer assisted methods, over 3000

different foods are analyzed and assigned a numerical point value.

These point values, some positive and some negative, are based on scientific analysis of 26 different components, 18 positive and 8 negative, of an individual food. Vitamins, minerals, fiber, fat, calories and other important components are measured.

In the past we selected food by the single category of how many calories it had. More recently we could tell how many fat grams a food contains. I'm not going to elaborate on the complete **Nutripoint** method of food selection in this book. I will say that for the first time **Nutripoints** makes it possible for you to educate yourself about how beneficial or non-beneficial a particular food really is for you. Thanks to this book, making wise food choices is much easier.

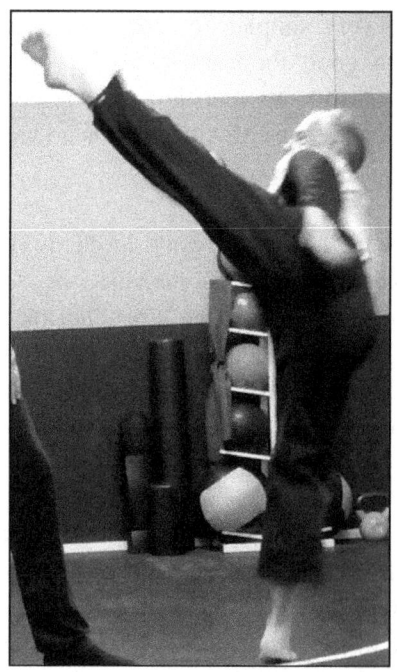

Most folks at age 63 are not too mobile. Eat good food and train regularly and you can do things most kids can't do.

SELF DEFENSE
VS
MMA

For the sake of simplicity, I'm going to use the term MMA (mixed martial arts) to refer to sport fighting contests in which a referee, a ring or Octagon or other prearranged area are used to fight.

MMA is the worlds fastest growing sport. There are numerous professional and amateur organizations for these contests. The UFC (Ultimate Fighting Championships) is the Undisputed Champ of these organizations. Other respected organizations include WEC, Strikeforce, Vale Tudo, shoot fighting, Pancrase, shooto, pit fighting, and so forth. While rules for these contests are minimal compared to tae kwon do, boxing, judo, karate, kickboxing, etc., there are still regulations protecting the fighters.

(L) UFC Hall of Famer and 5 time World Champion, Randy 'The Natural' Couture, and JD at Team Quest in Gresham, OR when Couture was Heavyweight Champ.
Evan Tanner

Even submitting by tapping out from a choke or joint lock is a luxury if a real bad guy or enemy is trying to hurt or kill you. There would be a shortage of contestants and an increase in blind cripples, if they just put two fighters in an enclosed area and said "The one who makes it out gets the money." Besides, I think that's against the law!

There are folks who forget that while MMA fights are much more realistic, as far as learning to protect oneself in a true self-defense situation than the previously mentioned boxing, tae kwon do, and other contests, there are still some very significant differences between self-defense and MMA sport fights. Experienced martial artists are aware of the differences but it seems like younger more impressionable folks get excited and don't consider some important factors.

Herb Steet using kenpo technique on JD. Ed Parkers style of karate is a very impressive self defense system, with many amazingly quick hands and low kicks.
Ray Ballinger

Among the main differences between the two types of

fighting is that in self-defense you are rarely allowed preparation time before you fight. There's no opportunity to warm up, stretch your legs, loosen your back and other muscles, before fighting.

You won't have a chance to physically or mentally prepare for the stresses encountered in a self-defense fight. There's no chance to plan your strategy like you would if you were in a MMA contest and knew something about your opponent. MMA contests require fighters to wear protective equipment; a mouthpiece, cup, gloves, hands & wrists wrapped and protected with tape.

'Little Fox' is currently a dance major at University of Oregon with a passion for teaching women's kick boxing and self-defense. She hits hard, especially for a little gal with New York modeling experience.   Kevin Launius/ The Daily Courier

Bare hands break frequently in street fights unless they have been conditioned. On the street, you may or may not be able to rely on your clothing for protection from injury. Some MMA fighters wear only very small shorts, leaving nothing to grab except a very sweaty person.

MMA fighters have worn a full judo-jujitsu or karate gi (uniform) to fight in, which can be used to throw or choke the person wearing the gi. The wearer can also use one's own gi to choke the opponent. On the street your coat or windbreaker can be used for or against you in the same manner as a gi top but, on the other hand, a heavy coat may offer some protection against knives and in some lucky cases have been known to protect wearers against smaller caliber gunshot wounds under certain conditions. There are instances of hollow point bullets from large caliber handguns being plugged up and not expanding because of heavy coats or layers of clothing.

Environmental differences are among the biggest differences between sport fighting in the arena and a self-defense fight. The mat in a ring or Octagon is mighty soft compared to concrete, asphalt or gravel and a wrestling double leg takedown would cause some nasty scraped knees if executed on the sidewalk or pavement. The lighting is excellent in MMA contests so you can count on seeing well. In self-defense many times the lighting is poor and sometimes you can hardly see because of night vision blindness. Go out of a

April with her surprise elbow at dusk.

Teresa practicing personal defense moves with Mike.   Grant Kirby

well-lit building into the night blackness and see how long it takes you to see well. Someone may even use bright light to make it hard for you to see them because they have positioned themselves so you must look into the sun or bright lights.

In an MMA contest, there are no objects to trip over, slip on, fall off, hide behind or use as a barrier and there's nothing to pick up and use as a weapon.

In self defense you won't have a corner man applying Vaseline to your face so you will be more resistant to cuts and punches will slide off your face easier. No coaches or training partners will be yelling instructions and encouragement or giving you water and refreshing ice during break time. If you start getting really pounded on and can't defend yourself, Big John McCarthy won't jump in and save you, and some bastard on the street may even kick you in the groin or knee you in the head when you are down!

I remember listening to Ed Parker at a seminar in the late 1970s. Someone asked him how many guys he could beat up. I could tell the questioner didn't know much about fighting, but Mr. Parker was understanding and his response was immediate, "What are they armed with?" He assumed someone out to harm him was going to have a weapon he would have to deal with in a real self-defense situation.

If some punk or thief confronts you on the street there's a good chance they could have a

JD with a low self defense kick to 'Thor' for those who think it's stupid to practice high kicking. Usually those folks just don't want to work hard enough to kick well.

buddy or partner in crime. I would hate to drag someone down to the concrete and put them in my guard Gracie jiujitsu style and have their buddy come up and start kicking, clubbing or stabbing me.

Time tested (for centuries) battle strategy and concepts for large scale military operations between warring countries are basically the same for small scale individual combat between 2 people. Rapid mobility, deception, effective weapons, fighting spirit and determination to defeat the enemy can apply to individual personal battles just as they applied to General

Schwarzkopf's battle plan when he made a 'Hail Mary' sweep and got the ground war off to a start in the first Gulf War.

Effective mobility (like Frankie Edgar used against BJ Penn) against one or especially multiple opponents is very important. Being on the ground is not the most mobile of positions. Using weapons that hurt the enemy from a distance without being close enough to be in danger is a basic warfare strategy that began when men threw sticks and rocks at each other. Kicking can enable you to reach an opponent with heavy power without allowing them close enough to reach you with their hands.

JD with kenpo simultaneous left hand checking, right hand finger whip to neck, and right foot groin kick, to long time friend and student Mr. David Massender.   Grant Kirby

Of course kicking can be dangerous to you for many reasons but if you practice kicking and surprise multiple opponents with your reach and power, stay mobile and evasive, it's harder to club or stab you than if you are down on the ground.

Even if you are legally armed with a firearm it's possible to be suddenly confronted with a knife or handgun at contact distance and it may be best to surrender your valuables quickly. Money can be replaced. Obviously it's better not to be surprised by being alert and not putting yourself in possible danger situations, but anyone can be surprised. There are very mean predatory people out there who shoot their victims after they have robbed them so they don't have a witness or just because they enjoy power over their victims.

6 year old Britini practicing knee strikes with her mother Lori.

Even if you are armed, you may need to use unarmed tactics to create distance or time to present your weapon. A solid front or sidekick can knock someone backward. If that doesn't end things, it should at least, slow them down long enough for you to present your weapon. Many shooting enthusiasts fail to realize this.

Many shooters don't bother with unarmed training methods because they believe they could prevail in most situations because they have a firearm. Someone could take a gun away from many of these people just because of their false sense of security. Just because they go to the range occasionally and shoot targets 25 yards away with a handgun they already have in their hand doesn't mean they can defend against a surprise at close range with their handgun in their holster, pocket or purse.

In self-defense, ice or snow may offer less than perfect footing. Strong winds and other sources of noise may prevent you from hearing as well as you normally would. Your clothing may be heavy or tight and restrict your movements. Your choice of shoes can make it difficult to maneuver and could affect which techniques you are able to use. If you are awakened out of a sound sleep by a home intruder, you are probably going to need a little time to get your mental faculties in gear, even if you can grab your shotgun, if you have one.

As you can see there are many variables in self-defense. Despite all the great and realistic things that have developed from the MMA contests, there is more to staying safe than some MMA people think about.

One of JD's fighters Nathan 'Monzon' Orchard delivers swing kick at opponent. The FCFF promoted a 'Civil War' type MMA event pitting Oregon State University (OSU) and the University of Oregon (U of O) to benefit OSU's wrestling team. Randy Couture - OSU and Chanel Sonnen - U of O, were alumni and honorary team captains for their teams. Good college fun! Mr. Orchard now teaches at his 10th Planet Jiujitsu in Portland OR. Below are some of the other MMA title belt holders JD trained.

'Captain' Chad Statten, JD, Nathan Orchard, Stephan 'Grizzly' Keen.

L to R.
Sean 'Iron Man' Miller age 40

Ernesto 'The Hammer' Duran

L to R.
Tim the 'Holocaust Kid' Sieg

'Tiger' Anthony Frye

STRENGTH TRAINING

OLD CHINESE PROVERB:
STRENGTH IS NOT EQUAL TO KNOWLEDGE. KNOWLEDGE IS NOT EQUAL TO TRAINING. WHEN YOU COMBINE KNOWLEDGE WITH TRAINING, THEN YOU HAVE TRUE STRENGTH.

Arron 'Thor' Maddron is an example of a powerful man who uses weight training to his advantage. He is a force to be taken seriously. 'Thor' asked JD how he could hit so hard.

There are different types of strength. Muscular, mental, and spiritual strength can all be cultivated and improved. This chapter will touch on the topic of physical strength training but the other types of training are just as important to a martial artist.

There are those who insist weight lifting is an absolute requirement to be strong. They believe technique training is important but whatever technique you use will be more effective because you will be stronger. There are those who don't lift weights but get their strength from other types of training. There's no question that if two fighters are equal in every way, except one is stronger than the other, the advantage goes to the stronger fighter.

That's a very difficult situation to find. Two fighters are very seldom exactly the same in technical skill, age, experience, knowledge and 'cardio' conditioning. A fighter who isn't much of a technician can certainly get by and win many fights because he simply overpowers average or less than average technicians.

A technician or technical fighter is one who has spent a great deal of time and energy developing their learned techniques. Martial arts teach movement, that if properly applied, will defend or attack with efficient results. I've seen great technicians I didn't believe would come out of a real scrap because they hadn't spent much time sparring or otherwise getting roughed up. With no experience in fighting competitions, they hadn't *really* learned what it's about to get punched, kicked, thrown, choked, joint locked or generally abused in the ring, Octagon or street. Of course, a martial artist has no business fighting on the street unless they have been attacked with no options remaining except to defend themselves.

Some of those technically superb martial artists look awesome during practice. They may kick straight up and have conditioning, speed and power. I don't know if they can take real punishment because they haven't been genuinely tested. Tested, to me, doesn't mean the tests at your school. Sparring at your school could be very rough and you could be plenty tough, but there's something about entering a competition with an opponent you know nothing about.

JD roundhouse kicking a larger, stronger man, Anthony 'Big Tony' Septinelli. High kicks to the temple in self defense rarely makes good sense but having the ability to do so makes lower self defense targets very easy to hit. Grant Kirby

Tested could also include surviving in combat and having to kill or be killed. Those who survive real combat are literally tested. Most of the time combat means using weapons on each other but that's another subject. It doesn't require much muscular strength to pull a trigger but it does require courage, stamina and mental strength to be under fire and still fight back.

Raw strength helps a fighter withstand and dish out punishment; it's a very good thing to have. However, too much emphasis on muscular strength development at the expense of technical development causes a fighter to over rely on his physical strength when genuinely tested. When two strength-based fighters compete the strongest usually wins.

Boxers - Time Tested Tough

The problem for a strength-based fighter comes when they meet a tough technical fighter. Boxing has been turning out tough fighters for over 100 years. It has a **much higher death rate** for fighters, and top level boxers earn **substantially more money** than UFC or other MMA fighters, so we need to learn from them. In 2010 at UFC 121, Brock Lesnar's $400,000 salary was the highest. Ali and Frazier each made $3,000,000 in 1971. I know that will change. MMA is just getting warmed up but facts are facts.

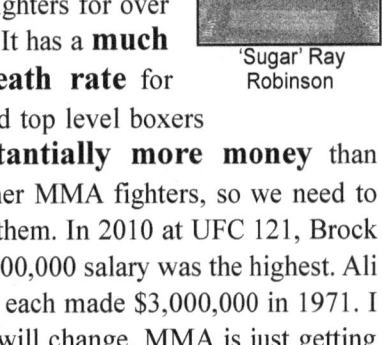

'Sugar' Ray Robinson

Manny Pacquiao with his record 7th, and now **8 weight division, World Titles**. He is a "big puncher" because he punches, but isn't a weigh lifter. Associated Press

Mayweather hitting Shane Mosley with a classic counter right cross. Mosley is the only man to beat De La Hoya twice, and is now business partners with him.   Jed Jacobsohn

'Sugar' Ray Robinson, who has been described as the *greatest pound for pound boxer ever*, didn't use weights to train. I know most young fighters don't care about ancient history, many believing they already know everything but **pay attention!** You will learn something.

P4P (pound for pound) Champion for almost a decade, Roy Jones Jr, or undefeated 6 weight division World Champ, Floyd Mayweather Jr, or the current P4P boxing Champ, **8 weight division** World Champion, Manny Pacquiao, are not weight lifters. Their hands are some of the best ever in professional boxing and they hit fast, hard and often.

A classic example of what a fluid, technically superb fighter can do to a stronger more muscular fighter, is what Muhammad Ali did to Big George Foreman. Ali didn't train with weights and earned **$6,000,000** for his fight in 1974. Ali made **$100,000,000** just for the merchandising rights to use his name. Remember the part about *pay attention* young MMA fighters? That's right, **One Hundred Million** Dollars.

Foreman knocking Frazier across the ring in their rematch.

Foreman flattening Norton

Ali's movements were more relaxed, fluid and smooth. His punches were delivered from the correct distance, with proper form and leverage, timed well and were fast and accurate. Study Ali in slow motion: You can really see how fluid and relaxed his punches are compared to his stronger, younger more muscular opponent.

'Smokin' Joe placed his autograph on Ali's butt in this photo.

Slow motion study clarifies the very different ways the two men deliver punches at each other.

For those who don't know, Foreman was World Heavyweight Champ in 1974. He won the Title the year before by knocking Joe Frazier down 6 times in 2 rounds. Joe always got up but the last time he got up, he needed help from the referee to find his corner and the fight was stopped.

Frazier had won the Title in the **'Fight of the Century'** in 1971, by knocking Ali on his butt in the 15th round, giving him his first professional loss. Foreman then destroyed Frazier. Ken Norton was the second man to defeat Ali breaking his jaw. Foreman flattened Norton in 2 rounds.

Foreman clobbered the only 2 fighters that had beaten Ali and the odds makers favored Big George. He had practiced cutting off the ring to keep Ali from dancing away but Ali let him pound on him while he leaned against the ropes. Slow motion study shows he pounded Ali hard, hitting him with tremendous punches as if he was pounding a heavy bag. Ali avoided or absorbed his powerful bombs and hit him back with crisp, smooth, accurate, well-timed punches. It's easier for opponents to see the looping arm punches Foreman relied on. He was accustomed to using his strength as he punched and his strength had enabled him to remain undefeated thus far, knocking out 37 of 40 opponents.

George had the highest percentage of knockouts of any Heavyweight Champion in Boxing History

Relatively inferior technical skills compared to Ali or not, this Foreman is a bad dude. From a technical standpoint, many times Foreman didn't have professional appearing boxing punches. Sometimes his punches seemed amateurish because he didn't use leverage. The term 'arm punches' in boxing refers to someone only using their arm power. A skilled fighter uses proper technique thereby maximizing his efficiency and power. Big George hadn't quite learned to take advantage of the real science and technique of boxing punching. He was so strong, he hadn't needed to

Foreman's jab

use proper form. His strength had been enough to smash everyone so far. Don't get me wrong; obviously there were plenty of things he did correctly. As Heavyweight Champ he must have done something right. He was very tough, and his jabs were good, probably the most underestimated punch he had.

Foreman sprawled on the floor

George's jab was delivered with technical skill, speed, and heavy power. It was usually his power shots that were delivered with his arms, and not his body. This is not pick on Mr. Foreman day. I just want to use this particular famous fight as an example of what

proper boxer strength training can accomplish, if one wants to be able to punch an opponent's lights out.

All those big strong muscles don't look nearly as impressive sprawled out on the floor, like Brock Lesnar was when Cain Velasquez whipped him in UFC 121. For those who are younger and only know about more recent fights, an example is James 'Sandman' Irvin after superb technical fighter Anderson Silva moved **UP** a weight class. He knocked the bigger and much stronger looking Irvin on his butt.

Anderson 'The Spider' Silva easily knocking out the larger more powerfully built James 'The Sandman' Irvin. Fight magazine I think

A few more punches while Irvin was down and the fight was over in seconds. During the pre-fight hype, Irvin self assuredly stated that 185 lb Silva couldn't come up to 205 lbs and beat him. "There's a reason why there are weight classes," Irvin said. "It wouldn't be fair." Wrong! After easily knocking Irvin senseless, Silva got down on his knees jiujitsu style and bowed to Irvin who just stood there appearing to not quite understand that type of display of respect. To be fair, perhaps, Irvin was just still discombobulated and seeing coo-coo birds.

Weight lifting is good for you; it makes you strong, healthy, feel and look good. Weight training can help rehabilitate an injury and develop strength in a weak area you may have. Weights helps you absorb body punishment, and if you are big and strong, help enable you to tackle and crush a smaller opponent who allows you to grab them.

The boxers considered to be THE GREATEST OF ALL TIME didn't train with weights. They trained to DELIVER POWER by punching someone. At the very tip top of the world's competition just a little difference may separate two fighters. I tell my students who want to lift weights all the advantages there are to weight training. I also tell them what happens to their bodies and neuromuscular systems when they spend too much time lifting weights. Weight lifting is different from weight training which is different from weight therapy.

One thing I do believe: The ***single most amazing feat in all of boxing history*** and probably all of sports history, is 45 year old George Foreman knocking out Michael Moorer (who had beaten Evander Holyfield) and regaining a World Heavyweight Championship **20 years after losing it** to Muhammad Ali.

Standing' next to Sugar' Ray Leonard when he was in his mid 40's. He looked to me, to be in his 20's.

To me, that's the most amazing accomplishment in all of sports but I attribute that amazing feat more to Foreman's spiritual strength and mental and physical toughness. This gave George the ability to absorb punishment and take a whipping most of the fight, not his physical strength. George landed a short right with his hips behind it, which was accurate and well timed and that was it for Michael Moorer that night. During the post fight interview a relieved Foreman made the remark "I thought I was going to have to belly bump him!"
Ya gotta love the guy!

After returning to boxing following a 10-year layoff as a preacher, Foreman hired

This is a photo of a poster that I asked these 2 Champions to autograph. When I showed the poster to George I told him I was a BIG fan of his, so I brought the biggest picture of him I could find. He said he was "Gonna get me for this." He signed it, "Thanks alot." Later Foreman made the most inspirational speech I have ever heard.

About 6 years later when I showed it to Ali, he looked at it and had a reaction like he dreamed of days before Parkinson's. He signed the poster and dated it 6 months into the future. These men are real life Heros to me and I am grateful for the excitement, inspiration and fighting education I have gotten from watching and reading about these **GREAT MEN**. This poster is now 36 years old.

Ali's Fighter Body

Ali's former trainer Angelo Dundee, for his comeback fights. Before the Ali fight, Dundee had predicted that Ali would knock Foreman out in the 9th or 10th round due to Foreman's muscularity tiring him out. Dundee was exactly correct but just one round late in his prediction. People with long time boxing experience know the pitfalls of developing excess tension with lifting muscles, *if you want to punch fast and hard.*

Worlds Best Hand Striker Training

When a significant amount of time is spent lifting weights, your muscles develop differently than if you spend your time punching grappling, or moving and lifting your own body like a gymnast. When asked, I tell people if you want to punch like a champ, you must practice like the Champs.

Regardless of what you or other weight lifting fans think, the Champs train the way they do for a reason. The very best boxers spend their time training their bodies to *deliver and avoid power,* **not have more strength.** If you spend your time shadow boxing in the air, the repetition develops the neuromuscular pathways necessary for firing a skilled technical punch, or combination of punches, with instantaneous reactions.

Fluid movements of men like Ali, 'Sugar' Ray Robinson and Leonard, Joe Louis, Roberto Duran, Roy Jones Jr, Floyd Mayweather Jr, Manny Pacquiao or other All Time Great boxers, were a result of throwing countless punches over the years. During training for the Pacquiao vs De La Hoya fight, those fighters paid assistants to count their **6000 punches per practice.**

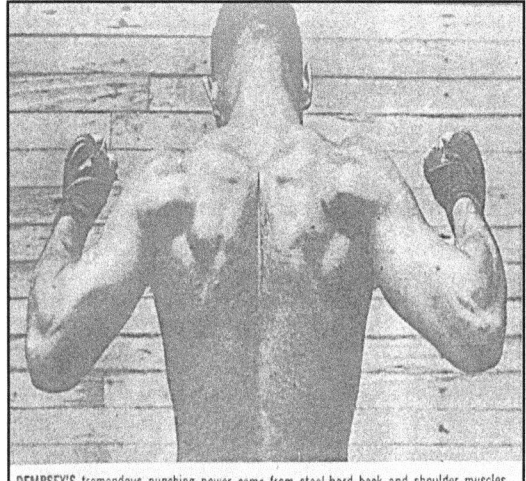

Jack Dempsey and the powerful punching muscles in his back.

OK, that's how the guys making **Tens of Millions of Dollars** per fight train to knock out their opponent.

Those men also spent considerable time learning and practicing being effectively mobile and positioning their bodies to be in and out of range quickly. They trained to time their punches and capitalize effectively on very brief openings their opponent presented them.

Effective mobility is difficult and needs constant practice. Time standing stationary lifting weight or at a weight machine or flipping a big rope doesn't contribute to effective mobility. Mobility is moving around. **Effective Mobility** is moving well with good balance, so you don't get hit, yet are able to instantly counter or take advantage of an opening. Chuck Liddell's wide stance movement is an example.

Watching massively strong Brock Lesnar stumble down and pirouette across the Octagon against Velasquez with his very strong legs but uncoordinated feet is an example of lack of effective fighting mobility practice. Those big guys don't like to move all that mass in practice. It's hard!

Ali strength training for his rematch with the powerful and superbly conditioned Ken Norton who broke his jaw in the first fight. Ali got into trouble with his Deer Lake, PA training camp neighbors for chopping down too many trees.

The strength and general conditioning training of Muhammad Ali and Oscar De La Hoya included chopping many trees. An ax only weighs a few pounds but the repetition of swinging it repeatedly develops the body's muscles differently. The torque of the hips into the horizontal swing of the ax uses hip power very similar to the hip torque during punching.

Forcefully exhaling out your nose or clenched teeth with each swing of the ax works your abdominal muscles. Each forceful exhalation has a similar value as an abdominal crunch, as far as working your belly. Ali read about Jack Dempsey developing his powerful back and shoulders from working as a lumberjack.

In 1919 Dempsey brutalized Heavyweight Champion Jess Willard, who was 5" taller and 48 lbs heavier. That little guy knocked the Champ down 5 times in the first round and gave Willard a beating like you won't see in the UFC. Dempsey's punching power knocked out many of Willard's teeth, broke his cheekbone and several of his ribs.

Big George chopping wood after his return from a 10 year boxing retirement to be a preacher.

33

'Homicide Hank'

Henry 'Homicide Hank' Armstrong owns a boxing record that will never be equaled. He won the 126 lb World Championship, the 147 lb, then the 135 lb Titles. All of this was done while he maintained the other titles. According to Bert Sugar, during a 2 year period (1937-38) Armstong won 27 of 27 fights with 26 KO's.

He's been the only man to own 3 World Titles simultaneously. During that period he also nearly won a middleweight 160 lb title. If he had won that fight, Armstrong would have been World Champion in ***half the weight divisions in boxing*** at the time.

Today in pro boxing, there's a 130 lb division between 126 and 135 and a 140 lb division between 135 and 147 lbs. Now there are 5 weight classes instead of 3, from 126 to 147 pounds. Modern rules require giving up one weight division title to be champion of another weight division.

Armstrong credited his nonstop fury in the ring to his earlier years working on the railroad, driving iron spikes in the ground. He wrote that he loved to swing the sledgehammer and pound those spikes. That work developed his back, shoulders, abdominal, forearms, wrists and hand strength. He also enjoyed running alongside the tracks when other workers rode the cart.

When swinging the sledge or ax, if you exhale forcefully as if you were punching, you will be amazed at the abdominal workout. If you wear a mouthpiece with a slit in the front for breathing, you can clench your teeth and practice exhaling that way. This repeated exhalation, will help you breathe correctly when you need to, without conscious effort like Jerry Quarry in the Breathe chapter.

These strength-training methods are useless for city dwellers. An old large tire placed on the ground and hit with a sledgehammer is now a fairly common practice, but few know its origins. Splitting firewood, hitting a big tire or tree stump with a sledgehammer for 2 hours like Ken Norton Sr did, works also. Splitting wood may be best because you have to be more focused and accurate with each downward swing and you should be picking up and tossing pieces of wood in various ways and directions, adding to the overall workout.

Unless you have access to private land in the country, you will get into big trouble chopping down someone's trees. You can get a bat with sliding weights on it like major league baseball players use to warm up. If you hang up a smaller tire to hit, like chopping a tree down, you can sort of duplicate the motion. It takes longer than just a few minutes to get a real workout with a light weight, but stay with it and swing hard and you will feel the results. Swing on both sides, and lead with your hips.

Both of these methods involve swinging 3-8 lbs for an extended time. Unless you spend the time doing it you won't get the idea at all. The first time you try it, your muscles will wonder what you did to them. You need to swing the ax or sledge hard because anyone can just coast along. Homicide Hank swung the sledgehammer all day working on the railroad, so he couldn't have gone quite as fast as you should if you train for 5 rounds. Remember this is supplemental, not primary training, so don't skip the technical training because it's more difficult.

'Smokin' Joe watching his son Joe Jr. warm up in the locker room before Jr. fights.

No pushups for Smokin' Joe Frazier

After beating Ali in 1971, I watched 'Smokin' Joe Frazier as a guest on a TV talk show. The host gave Frazier a playful grab on the upper arm, then remarked that his bicep was sort of soft, in a non-insulting way, just a surprising observation. Frazier said he wanted relaxed, smooth punching muscles not hard muscles. The host said that he thought the Champion of the World would want rock hard muscles and be doing pushups and other hard muscle making activities.

Ken Norton skipping rope

'Smokin' Joe said he couldn't do a push up, that he *punched* when he worked out. The host said he didn't believe Joe Frazier couldn't do a pushup. They nearly got into an argument about Joe's ability to do a pushup. I'm sure he could do a push up but I was amazed at Frazier's absolute insistence that he didn't want to develop hard muscles, he wanted smooth punching muscles.

This is a funny photo to me. During the Super Stars Competitions, bowling was one of the events. Norton is getting cocky with 'Superfoot' Wallace. I have personally seen what unhuman things he could do with his left foot. Norton has no clue what Wallace is capable of, regardless if Norton is a former Heavyweight Champion.

In the early 1970s I enjoyed watching the Super Stars Competitions on Wide World of Sports. The show featured many top athletes from a multitude of sports competing in events that were varied and different from the sport each athlete excelled in. This type of competition gave a view of an athlete's overall athletic ability.

At the time, Bob Seagren was the Worlds best pole vaulter. He weighed about 170 lbs and military pressed 220 lbs for this competition. Joe weighed about 220 lbs but couldn't military press 170 pounds. He struggled hard to lift that weight up but was unable. Nobody laughed at Frazier that I could see; apparently they thought he might knock their head into outer space. During some swim races in the pool, I thought Frazier might drown but again nobody laughed at him. So what did these "old guy" memories teach me? It made me start to realize and be acutely aware of sport specific training nearly 40 years ago

JD finishing an 11 mile cross country race averaging less than 7 minute per mile time. 'Super' Dan Anderson explained that if I wanted to kick like he did, I should spend that running energy practicing kicks. I started kicking a lot more, and rarely ran. **Kicking is a lot more work.**

Sport Specific Training

Sport specific training: What does that really mean? A simple question I pose to those who ask is, "How does an Olympic runner train? What's your answer? A typical response I receive is "They run." I say, "Well, how far?" They give varied answers. What's your answer?

I tell them I asked a trick question. Which event does the Olympic runner compete in? Does he run the 100, 200, or 400-meter dash? Each of these events requires different focus and training methods to win at the Olympic level. There are men such as Usain Bolt who compete in several of these similar distances successfully but they still train slightly differently for each event. Does that Olympic runner race in the 5,000, or 10,000-meter races or does he run the marathon?

I did my best to run behind this woman for another 11 mile race but couldn't come close to keeping up with her. Frustrated and wondering why for 11 miles, I am finding out here that she *trains* for marathons.

Dawn Welch

Olympic runners competing in the 100-meter dash and the marathon will share very few training methods, except putting one foot in front of the other. The difference is that in a race, one will be taking much longer, faster strides for less than 10 seconds, the other will be taking smaller strides for a couple of hours. Running is a relatively simple, noncomplex event.

No, I don't think running is easy. I ran 24 miles for my 24th birthday and that hurt. Nor do I believe it's easy to be the best runner. There's much more to being a winning runner than meets the eye. Champion runners need running technique, strategy and other skills to win. Compare that to a combination of kicks and punches delivered quickly, accurately and at the correct time, when an opponent is doing their best to knock you out. Running is very, very basic, very simple.

Royce Gracie (R) dosen't look very tough but he sure made believers out of many larger, stronger men with his technical skill. Black Belt magazine

Ask a runner to do some of the technical skills used by a kick boxer. The flexibility, coordination, balance, reflexes and complex neuromuscular requirements baffle a runner. I repeat, running isn't easy by any stretch of the imagination. The idea is, that even in a very basic, much less physically complex activity, such as running, there are specific training methods used to stay competitive in their respective events.

Developing Tense Muscles

Carlos Monzon held the Middleweight World Title for a record 7 years and 14 title defenses, until Bernard Hopkins beat his record. This skinny guy was undefeated his last 83 fights. Not just a champion, he was among the best of all time, in a crowded weight class.

The difference in the way weights develop muscles compared to fighting, and especially punch training methods, is that during weight lifting, muscles are trained to be tense. While lifting a weight, muscles are tensed until you get the weight up for that particular lift. While lowering the weight, the muscles preventing the weight from falling are tensed for the time needed to lower the weight.

It takes a few seconds to get that weight up, a few more to lower it. Then you perform more repetitions for more seconds. More sets, more reps, *more time* training the muscles *to be tense*. All of this is GREAT for making strength but not firing a punch. Punching does not require muscle tension for any longer than a brief explosion of energy, directed at *only* the exact muscles making the fist flash to the target, to deliver one of a multitude of different punches.

Hapkido hand techniques allow you to take the initative and control the situation. Applied properly you can put the hurt on someone. Waiting until punches start flying makes it hard for most to grab a wrist or hand. This is JD and 'Thor'.

Any additional muscular tension while that fist is on its way to its intended target, results in a braking action to the punch. Excess muscle tension creates more exertion than necessary. One punch delivered with excess tension won't tire you. Numerous punches demand more oxygen and will sap your strength. George now agrees.

That fight is just one, but it's a famous classic example of excessive muscular exertion, attributed *directly to the training of his muscles to be tense*. Mr. Foreman was 25 years old and *in magnificent physical condition*. There's no reason a World Champion athlete in the prime physical condition of his life, should tire out in the 8th round unless he lacked sport specific training. The UFC's powerful Shane Carwin gassing out early from beating on Brock Lesnar during the first round, is another more recent example.

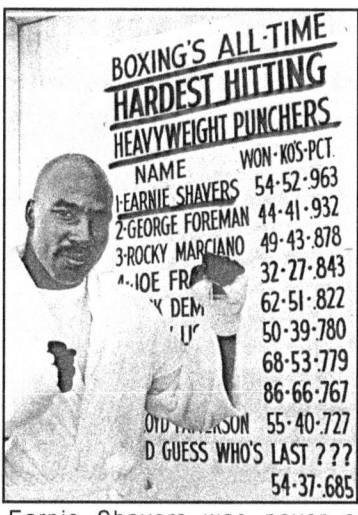
Earnie Shavers was never a champion, but sure had a punch. He retired with 74 wins with 68 KO's. His type of training is below.

Every day except Sunday, the schedule was the same, beginning with a 3-5 mile run at 6:00 in the morning. Shavers and his sparring partners pursued the same routine until mid-afternoon. At that point Shavers continued his workout, while his sparring partners went to lick their wounds. Compare the schedules:

	SHAVERS		SPARRING PARTNERS
6:00	3-5 mile run	6:00	3-5 mile run
6:30	Agility excercises	6:30	Agility excercises
7:30-12:00	Breakfast, short rubdown, rest	7:30-12:00	Breakfast and back to bed
12:30-2:30	Workout and sparring sessions	12:30-2:30	Workout and sparring
3:00-5:30	Swim, chop wood	3:00-4:00	Steambath to ease the body pains; swim
6:00	Dinner	4:00-7:00	Free
7:00-8:30	Relax, watch fight films, etc.	7:00	Dinner
8:30-9:15	Oil rubdown	8:00-On	Free
9:30	Sleep		

Coordinating Muscles with the Brain

Part of the process of sport specific training, for a punching technician, is the harmony and coordination between his brain and muscles. A technician's brain and muscles are involved in delivering many different punches, defensive movements, footwork and reflexive movements. A fighter is faced with the most complex of tasks; coordinating his mental and physical power, and all of this must be done in fractions of a second.

A fighter must first see and recognize an attacking technique, then respond appropriately in either an offensive or defensive manner. After interpreting the opponent's attack, a choice of techniques to use is needed. Fighters have favorites, but there are usually several responses for countering a particular attacking technique.

A great fighter must have a mind able to quickly interpret the opponent's movements and respond with correct choices for each of the opponent's techniques. He must do all of this in parts of a second and change direction, technique or speed, instantly according to information his eyes, or other sensors relay to his brain.

Arron 'Thor' Maddron is obviously a very powerful man whose focus is bodybuilding. His background in gymnastics gives him surprising flexibility, coordination and quickness. His attitude, training with JD, is always polite, respectful and courteous. It's always a pleasure to train with him. JD is thankful to him for his help with the photos and video.
Pump magazine

This is where sport specific training experience helps. Years of being in the various situations countless number of times, helps the brain speed up the multitude of selection choices, while at the same time, allowing other muscles not needed for each exact movement, to be relaxed.

Muscle irradiation is when the brain fires off too many signals at too many muscles. Irradiation is a big word for too much muscle tension. It's sort of like the brain firing massive numbers of spam e-messages off to area nerves and muscle fibers, as opposed to a much smaller number of e-messages focused to more specific muscles. There are those unable to grasp the importance of this fact. That's fine, they don't have to.

There are those who insist that even Bruce Lee lifted weights. He did, but not very much, and he felt he needed to strengthen his small half Chinese frame. Some weight training won't ruin you and eventually everyone needs to strengthen a body part that's weaker or injured.

A program to address those weaknesses or injuries with weights is vitally important. This type of weight training is a controlled, safe method to help and improve you; which is different from pumping iron or machines to get overall body strength.

Roy Jones Jr beating up Clinton Woods while **forcefully exhaling** thru the slit in his mouthpiece as described in the Breathe chapter. Rob Finch/ The Oregonian

HBO expert boxing analyst and trainer Emanuel Steward has trained many world champions including Thomas Hearns, Lennox Lewis and as of this writing Heavyweight World Champ Wladimir Klitschko. He calls a muscular, weight trained fighter who hits real hard a "Power Puncher."

A "Big Puncher," as described by Steward, is someone like 'skinny' technical puncher 6' 1" tall 147 lb. Thomas 'The Hitman' Hearns, who plastered many world champions, including Roberto Duran. Hearns had a **32-0 with 30 KO's record, for a 93% KO average** when he fought 'Sugar' Ray Leonard the first time. Undefeated and knocking out almost everyone, qualifies as Brutal Power to me. Steward also elaborates by saying the same things Angelo Dundee says about muscular development for boxers.

Oscar De La Hoya

Active Rest

Roy Jones Jr dominated boxing for nearly a decade, and was recognized as the P4P best in the world. He was World Champion at 160, 168, 175 lbs and beat up John Ruiz for a Heavyweight Championship. He has been described by some of boxing's most knowledgeable men to be among the greatest boxers ever, and I agree.

Consider a powerful man's hands or feet to be poison. Don't let their weapons touch you. Large opponents offer lots of target area. Speed, timing and accuracy make a larger man respect a smaller man's power and difficulty to hit. JD demonstrates a karate ridgehand on Anthony Septinelli. The UFC's Loyoto Machida KO'd Rashad Evans with a left ridgehand to win the 205 lb Title. Grant Kirby

Lifting your training partners in wrestling practice, will allow you to lift and slam him to the ground. Respect your training partners, it's their turn next. Grant Kirby

Roy Jones Jr had some of the fastest hands ever to put on gloves. His foot speed and effective mobility made most of his opponents look slow and clumsy in comparison. Roy says he did not lift weights; he punched. He also liked playing basketball for fun, which is the difference between those who goof off or party between fights, and a man who shows up to fight in absolutely fit condition. Running up and down the court, jumping, sprinting, stopping, changing direction and using his eyes and reflexes between fights, paid off for Mr. Jones in a big way.

Jones knew he would show up in shape, and perhaps his competitors have had more lay off time in between serious training for up coming fights. My wrestling coach 'Wild Bill' Ryder didn't like his wrestlers playing basketball because it's a good way to hurt your knees or ankles or get cut with an elbow, like Obama's lip was playing basketball recently. Any activity that tax's your body has a potential to cause you injury.

Randy Couture calls this or other similar types of training **"active rest."** At age 45, Couture would run 10 or more miles thru the Las Vegas desert for something different to do besides his regular training routine. He would do this for a mental break to stave off training boredom, except this activity is highly beneficial for his body.

Going out partying is not beneficial, which is why his body looks great and he is still beating up men in the Octagon at age 47. Despite 'The Natural' being an Inspirational Hero of mine, all his running means he doesn't kick so well.

So far, to my knowledge, Oscar De La Hoya is the biggest money making fighter of any type, ever in the world. He's another modern former champion who didn't lift weights as part of his workouts. I read that he had a shoulder injury years ago and was going to use weight training to rehabilitate his injury.

Great! Young fighters who are sort of skinny and need to put on some weight and strength can use moderate weight training also. Just remember, it should be supplemental, not primary training.

Once a fighter has matured to a certain age, they should practice punching and wrestling for strength development. Wrestling requires and develops more strength and conditioning than jujitsu. Wrestlers don't get the luxury of lying on their backs and relaxing. Wrestlers have to fight off their backs and that's harder.

Yes, MMA fighters or others wanting to defend themselves should learn jujitsu as I have. I'm just talking about strength now. Pick up your own body weight like a gymnast. Move yourself and you will be able to move your body well. Hard work ethics make you strong. Include many different activities and you will be strong for a long fight.

Watch Nature's tough animals. Do they lift weights or do they lift and move their bodies, and play fight or wrestle with each other? Does that chimpanzee with 98.77% the same DNA as you, but pound for pound about 7 times stronger than you, lift weights? Not in nature.

If you are a fighter with *striking efficiency* as your goal and you have 100 Energy Units to spend in a workout, spend them all practicing fighting related activities. A boxer can skip rope; a kick boxer can substitute rope work with even more different kicking drills from karate, Hapkido, or tae kwon do, to accomplish the legwork.

Do you think the kick boxer will suffer if he delivers extra kicks or mobility footwork practice, instead of skipping rope? No. If a striker takes those 100 Units and begins by light shadow boxing while moving and using his footwork to loosen up, is this is going to help him be mobile, balanced, fast and hard to hit? You bet.

Punching the speed bag, double end bag, the focus mitts, and the heavy bag, will consume many of those 100 Energy Units. If you go hard on those pads and bags, you will be tired or you are slacking. If you spar after you are tired like Ali would do, you should use up more of those Units. If you wrestle after that, you will be in superlative condition, able to pick up and slam down someone a whole lot bigger than you. How strong do you need to be?

Wrestlers are generally stronger overall and in superior physical condition than jujitsu fighters, but lack sneaky submission techniques that can end a fight quickly against the stronger wrestler. If you have completed the above activities with tough guys and are still feeling energetic enough to go lift some unnatural weights, then you aren't giving "Big Puncher" training your all.

Remember, if you want to end a fight quickly, watch the master technicians pop a well-timed, accurate punch or kick to their opponent and watch them crumple. A recent example of that is the simple counter right hand BJ Penn cracked (speed, timing, accuracy) the larger, more powerfully built Mr. Matt Hughes with, in UFC 123.

Compare that to a ground and pound brawl between 2 powerfully built, strong men trying to overpower and bash each other, such as Tito Ortiz and Ken Shamrock used to do. Brawlers and wrestlers, lacking in technical standup striking skills or submissions, are examples of that type of energy expending, punishment receiving method.

That method is less effective at quick endings to a fight. Remember the Japanese judo saying SIERYOKU ZENYO, which translates to maximum efficiency with minimum effort.

The hard part is the training!

Mr. Leon Rogers' Century Martial Arts Team

ATTACKING THE BALANCE

Among the best things about wrestling and especially judo practice, is learning to attack an opponent's balance.

JD is about 185 lbs and Thor is 100 lbs heavier and considerably stronger. If you have any questions about whether these throws work, Thor will assure you they do.

If this were concrete instead of a mat Thor is about to fall on, there's a high risk of serious injury to a very powerful man. A skilled fighter knows proper falling and rolling skills.

If you want to be a good fighter and have never had formal judo practice, you should. Judo is a sport lacking in many ways for serious street fighting because rules prohibit punches, kicks, head butts, eye gouges and ripping the throat, etc.

Despite that, judo is an excellent way to learn many other important aspects of fighting. You are taught that there are 3 parts to a judo throw: First is *off balance*, second is *entry* and third is *execution*. Proper execution of a throw requires your opponent to be a little off balance (either of you can cause it) then you must enter in or position your body for the throw you are attempting.

The execution of the judo throw itself is usually quite easy, sometimes amazingly easy, provided you have done the first 2 things correctly. I will be the first to say that many judo throws are not street oriented but others are *absolutely devastating* to an opponent if the throw is executed correctly at the proper time.

A skilled martial artist can deliver many powerful kicks and strikes to protect himself in self-defense. These techniques aren't allowed in judo but there are some judo throws that are very much a part of my street defense because they can work so well. Other factors making a judo throw so devastating, is throwing an opponent onto concrete or something else hard and painful to land on.

In addition, some judo throws make it possible to land on your opponent as you throw him. By

JD about 1974 practicing judo reaping throw. Four decades of practice makes these throws instantly available for use, if their body position and distance is correct.

practicing judo throws at judo practice, everyone develops favorite throws, just as you have your favorite techniques in any other style of fighting art. Once you gain a feeling of comfort and ease executing some of your favorite throws, if an opponent is close, throws *just seem to happen* for you.

Throws work especially well in self defense situations if the bad guy is not used to being close to a skilled judoka. Throwing someone who is not highly skilled at falling, onto concrete and landing on him with your body weight, usually means they will be seriously injured. Ribs are easily broken and can puncture their lungs or heart which will be fatal.

Jump kicking and lots of judo hopping drills allow JD's legs to be strong enough to lift nearly 500 lbs with just 1 leg, but only for an instant, then the weight is gone as the reaping throw is completed.

Some of these basic throws make for extremely efficient results per expenditure of your energy. I have cracked my share of judo opponent's ribs by accidentally landing on them in competition. I have never tried to purposely cause injury to anyone, in any type of fighting competition and neither should you but if you are a serious competitor, sometimes injuries occur.

It makes a believer out of you when you throw someone skilled at falling techniques, to a soft mat and witness them writhing in pain after you executed a quick, easy-to-do judo throw but accidentally landed hard on them. Those sights and sounds make me think of what would happen to an unskilled person thrown to the asphalt. It's impressive. Be careful with your training partners. Remember they throw you next!

This is an example of stopping your weight before it smashes a valuable training partner. As stated before, if 'Thor' were a real bad guy about to land on concrete, all your weight is very simple to add to the damage. In fact, it's much easier to land on them hard, than to stop your weight.

With time at real judo practice, you can throw someone quickly and easily without thought. You get that unconscious, effortless feeling with a kick or punch as well. Your hands or feet will fire-off on their own and land when someone comes into them. The result is quite effective and surprising to both of you.

Timber 'Little Fox' Ogden thinks it's a trick because JD went over so easily with her first shoulder throw

I have won judo matches by Ippon (full point, match over) and didn't know what happened until the referee pointed to me saying IPPON! The first time this happened I remember asking my first judo instructor Mr. Bill Foster "What happened? He laughed and told me what throw I used to win.

That's the goal of a martial arts technique; to execute the movement without conscious thought, because your body has learned to feel and execute the movement by reflex action. In judo or wrestling it's by body feel - a very memorable experience.

JD being shoulder thrown in martial arts practice while wearing his boxing shirt in the late 1970s.   Grant Kirby

In Japanese, **ju** means gentle and **do** means way: Judo, the gentle way. Its underlying principle is not to resist the direction they want to take you. Let them go there by throwing them with their own momentum or strength and your technique. The ability to throw someone quickly and effectively makes you feel all the judo practices were worthwhile. All the break fall practice, getting thrown by your partners, bumps, bruises, mat burns, getting choked, your joints locked. All that sweat was worth it.

Judo is a sport invented by Jigaro Kano. His goal was to borrow some of the less dangerous techniques from jujitsu and create a sport that people can safely compete against each other without risking injury from the deadly techniques. Japanese jujitsu appears quite different from Brazilian style juijitsu, popularized by the Gracie family.

Early 1970s holding down an opponent for another win in judo competition. At first, those sneaky ('cheating' to a wrestler) submissions that judo/jujitsu guys used, were unfamiliar and they caught me a lot. After time and practice learning submission defense, the wrestling conditioning, balance, strength and hustle began to work on them.

I wholeheartedly believe the judo, aikido, Hapkido type falling and rolling practice is worth its weight in gold for injury avoidance. Rolling and falling skills can help you in many situations which have *absolutely nothing to do with a fight.*

Accidents, slips and falls from many situations, can go from something that could cause you injury or even death, to nothing more than a quick roll and pop up to your feet. Some students don't enjoy

Kristy Lee Cook practicing diving rolls, going from her right shoulder diagonally across her back to come up on her left rump cheek. This can save your life. This gal is quite an athlete, and she can kick, punch, grapple and shoot. It's just a shame the poor gal is so darn homely! :-)

rolling and falling practice. I tell them I have used rolls and falls more in real life situations outside of training than **anything else in all my martial arts training.** Retired Marine, Major Lee Frakes, says each time you are thrown or fall in practice and hit the mat with force, it makes you that much stronger.

My Kenpo instructor Mr. Herb Steet, was riding his motorcycle and a car turned in front of him. He was hit and thrown 60 feet through the air but he avoided death by doing a martial arts roll. He lost his lower leg, suffered other severe injuries, but recovered and continued teaching martial arts. A proper roll or fall, done reflexively because of training, could save your life!

Choking, joint locks, grappling and basic throws are essential to a well-rounded fighter. Practice judo so you can go after an opponent's balance; you will be surprised at its effectiveness. Without balance, an opponent usually has little chance to get set and hurt you. If you fight a superior stand up fighter, you develop the confidence and ability to attack his balance.

A disadvantage to throwing an opponent in self-defense could be that he has a friend who wants to thump on you if you stay on the ground very long. I think many grappling based fighters are accustomed to sport contests. They have a tendency to ignore this street defense possibility.

Ground tactics are a disadvantage in a multiple attack situation. Remember this if you focus too much on grappling. If you are self-defense oriented, you need good footwork and evasive hit and move tactics, especially against multiple opponents. Muhammad Ali said "He who hits and moves away, lives to fight another day."

There's no substitute for real judo practice where judo is all you do. The constant practice and thinking like a judoka, is the only way to really have those throws work instantly when you need them. It's not the same to simply practice some judo throws occasionally with training partners. You don't have to spend the rest of your life only doing judo but you should concentrate on judo for a while so you can count on your friend **gravity,** when you toss an opponent.

THE BASICS

Former Top Rated Karate fighter, Kirby Barker, uses a simple lead hand strike to JD. Anyone who dismisses 'point' karate has not trained with top notch black belt karate fighters. All martial arts styles have disadvantages, but if you want to learn to fight, you should look to karate for it's good points.

Herb Steet

Grappler JD had a learning curve when fighting International caliber black belt fighters like 'Mr. Bill' Rooklidge. Being stronger, and in better shape, was not enough to defend against quickness and technique. 'Mr. Bill' became my friend and helped me learn to strike like he did.

Herb Steet

Knowing 5,000 techniques from a few styles won't prepare you if someone surprises you in a fight with moves you've never seen before. A well-schooled martial artist who is serious about self protection needs a complete and thorough understanding of basics from many different schools of thought. This is especially true if they want to compete in MMA.

You must be familiar with and ready for, techniques that don't look like what everyone at your school or gym does. What about people who don't train the way you do; how do they move?

When someone proficient at other styles delivers unfamiliar techniques at you, what does it look like? Find someone who excels at another style to train with, not a beginner or intermediate. Don't think a kick boxer can zoom in and grab you in a double leg take down the same as an experienced wrestler can. Just because a kick boxer practiced with some buddies who exchanged methods, doesn't mean he will show you what a real double leg looks and feels like.

That exchange of information and techniques will certainly be better than not having a clue what wrestlers can do but if you really want to know and be prepared, find wrestlers to show you what they can and can't do.

It's much better now but many people who train in the martial arts still don't want to leave their *'comfort zone.'* They have an especially difficult time doing something differently, especially if they have spent a long time in a system or style and don't like feeling inept at another method. A black belt in judo may not enjoy learning to kick or punch because

'Superfoot' went Undefeated as a full contact karate fighter. Wallace is a wrestler who badly injured his right knee practicing judo, and then focused on kicking with his left foot. Here he nearly decapitates his opponent who moves into his hook kick. Black Belt Magazine

Before the UFC, not everyone knew about a basic rear naked choke. Now almost everyone knows it. They may not know it's called 'naked', because jujitsu practioners wear gi tops to throw and choke each other, and this choke is used without the top, or... naked.

he has to go from being an expert, back to being a less accomplished rookie.

If the judoka has grown accustomed to having others admire and look up to him for his judo skills developed from years of dedicated practice, he may have trouble starting over learning new kicks. Few people seem to be able to humble themselves and look like a beginner. That's what it takes; you have to start somewhere, and looking like a rookie is par for the course.

The best fighters stick to the basics of fighting but have more speed, deception, timing, angles and little variances and personal modifications in how they execute simple basics. The 'little' things are what separate the best from the very good. How do those 'best' fighters get those enhanced simple basic abilities?

They practice for years, never getting so good that the fundamentals are overlooked. They don't just learn basics, then spend their time on techniques that the 'advanced' fighters are supposed to practice.

For example, everyone who fought Ali knew he had a fast left jab. Was Ali's jab a secret technique, a never before seen mystery move? No, but some of his opponents didn't see many of those jabs whacking their face because Ali's hand was too fast. The jab was the same as they'd seen before, just faster. A properly

I like to practice with big strong men like 'Thor'. It makes regular sized people seem smaller, and prepares me for their strength.

delivered boxing jab is an extremely effective weapon but not a secret.

Joe Frazier had a vicious left hook that was also no secret and he used it to plant Ali on his butt in the first of their 3 fights. Did Ali know Frazier had a wicked left hook from Hell? Yes, but Frazier used that basic punch really well.

Cassius Clay jabs Sonny Liston with proper form. Studying this man is where I learned much of my boxing basics. 1964 AP Photo

Bill Wallace only used 3 kicks with his lead left foot; side, roundhouse and hook kicks. He used 2 punches with his left hand; a jab and a hook, yet he remained undefeated in Full Contact Karate. Did his opponents know he used 3 kicks and 2 punches? Yes, but he worked on those basic kicks and punches until people couldn't deal with them. Again, there's nothing secret about the handful of Wallace's kicks or punches. He used his rear right hand for defense.

For those of you who don't know or may be thinking Bill Wallace is ancient history because we now have the UFC, I suggest you go to YouTube and watch a 10 round exhibition kick box match between Wallace age 45 and his friend Joe Lewis, age 46. Compare the technical striking skills Wallace displays in that match to what you see today. Most of what Wallace does with his left foot is missed because his foot is too quick. Thru 2010 not one fighter has equaled his technical striking ability in the UFC.

'Smokin' Joe with a leaping left hook in the 15th round to knock Ali down and win the **20th Centurys biggest fight**. Joe autographed his right foot for me.

One can apply lessons from ring fighters to real personal survival situations. Basics are the building blocks; remove them and everything else falls apart. Make a basic mistake in the ring and you could be waking up wondering why all those people are standing over you looking all concerned. Make a basic mistake in a real battle and they could be splitting up your gear and putting you in a body bag.

Practice fundamentals; never get past them. Just learn more simple basics from other effective arts. Recent MMA open mindedness has helped tremendously but generally, stylists have a way of dismissing the importance of an aspect of fighting they don't practice much, if at all, in their particular style. For example, over the years I have talked with many boxers with a low opinion of the effectiveness of kicks. Many boxers believe they can wade right through any kick someone aims at them and punch their lights out.

Joe Lewis with a simple lead hand strike at JD.
George Boyle

That could happen to a mediocre kicker or if a boxer has trained with good kickers and knows what to watch out for. Experience dealing with kicks makes a huge difference. It allows a boxer to recognize, react and defend against kicks that would ordinarily surprise someone lacking that experience. After some training, the best way to learn is to jump in there and learn in competition. If you have a positive attitude, you should be happy to have taken part in the event and you will know much more after each experience. Kickers, who haven't trained with boxers underestimate what a smooth boxer with good footwork can do by evading or jamming a kick and then punching them fast, hard and often.

Good boxers are tough; some are very, very tough. Some boxer's best defense is to have their opponent pound on them and punch themselves into exhaustion. A pro boxers' fantastic conditioning methods and being accustomed to frequent poundings during sparring sessions give them the ability to absorb punishment most people could never dream of taking. Randall 'Tex' Cobb took a beating from Larry Holmes that was so bad it caused Howard Cosell to quit being a boxing commentator. When asked about that beating on a TV talk show, Cobb

Ali about to collapse from beating on Chuck Wepner. The ref is stopping the fight, and Ali is sagging. This fight inspired Slyvester Stalone to write the movie **'Rocky.'** Some guys are Real Tough and can take a brutal pounding.

responded calmly and in a matter of fact manner, **"To tell you the truth, I didn't think his hands could take that kind of abuse!"**

'IMAX' Doug age 70, delivers a basic rear uppercut, lead hook combo to 'Pistol' Pete. Working the basics is easier on your body when you are a bit older.

Many inexperienced strikers who haven't learned yet believe they can prevent a wrestler from zooming in and dragging them down. If the striker hasn't had experience with grapplers shooting in on them, they could be looking up at the sky, in a painful position, wondering what happened so fast. Most wrestlers don't know what it's like to shoot face first into a good boxer's uppercut, or a kick boxer's knee strike, or get their neck stuck in a jujitsu guillotine choke.

The faster and more forcefully a wrestler closes that gap when shooting in for the takedown, the worse it hurts, providing the striker keeps the correct distance, maintains their balance, and strikes with accuracy. Failure to do these things to a wrestler-grappler type, can lead to a very brief sinking feeling and then you hit the deck with them on top. They are all basics just from different methods; all are effective provided they are done properly.

Wrestlers may underestimate judo-jujitsu chokes or joint locks. As an experienced wrestler, my early experiences against judo competitors in 1973 were very favorable. The conditioning, balance, strength and techniques developed from years of wrestling worked great! The problem was when I tried to go after the good black belts who were well versed in those 'cheating' (in wrestling) chokes and joint locks.

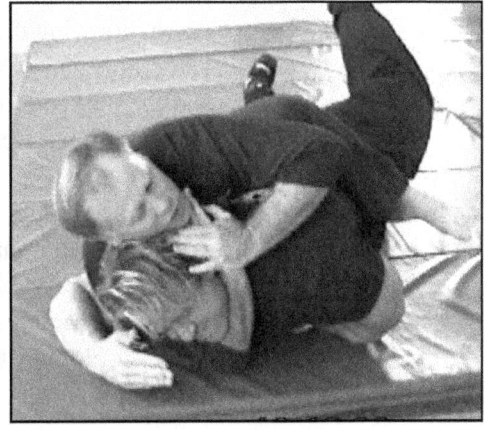

My favorite submission is the one that's presented to me but a wrestling surfboard, with a rear naked choke, is very high on the list. 'Thor' is a great sport!

I wasn't used to submissions and had no idea how to defend against them. Excellent wrestler, Ken Shamrock, was a quick victim of Royce Gracie's side choke in their first UFC fight. Apparently, Ken hadn't yet experienced a real choking technician and it was an easy fight for Royce. However Shamrock did his homework after that first fight and was more prepared next time.

Amber is a gal who would hurt many men badly even if they knew she had been trained. Don't try to start something with her!

The next time they fought, it was officially a draw but by looking at the two after the fight, Royce's cheek bone appeared busted and Ken looked fine. I read things Mr. Shamrock said later about that fight, that were somewhat disrespectful toward Royce. Proud fighters hate to fight to a draw, especially when you beat up the guy, but I would remind Mr. Shamrock that Mr. Gracie could have killed him easily in their first fight. All Royce had to do was keep that choke on him a few seconds longer and Ken would have been unconscious. Holding the choke on after they are out deprives the brain of oxygen and causes death. In a REAL NO RULES fight Shamrock could have been killed.

Mr. Shamrock did display maturity and grace when Tito Ortiz beat him soundly in their third fight. Few things are worse in fighting competitions than a disrespectful, sore loser.

Big strong men may underestimate a slightly built Chinese stylist. The little person may be able to poke out an eye, rip a throat or break a knee before the big strong guy has a chance to clobber the little skinny guy. The little guy may appear very harmless to a much bigger, stronger man who may be over confident and never gets in gear to crush the little guy.

That can work for women also. Conventional thinking for many people is that most women are not expected to be very tough. I know they can be! I'm just taking the uneducated position for a minute saying there are many men who can't picture a woman thumping them. They will probably have their mental guard down, allowing the woman the chance to get in a good strike to a vulnerable spot. Once that technique has been properly delivered and the guy is in major pain she can then run away, or follow up with additional techniques, then get away.

The pregnant Pam demonstrates the front kick, another important basic strike with lots of power and reach. Anderson Silva made a believer out of Vitor Belfort with it. Her 2 other kids treat her with respect.

If the big strong person had been forewarned of the woman's skills or didn't underestimate their smaller opponent the little person or woman may not stand a chance. Even when forewarned, many large, strong people still can't believe a 'little twerp' could hurt them. Use that to your advantage if you aren't big and powerful in appearance.

The small Chinese stylist or smaller woman could make a mistake due to their false sense of skills and ability and one punch from the strong person could knock them cold or kill them. As a rule, a slightly built person can't take such punishment from a powerfully built man who punches reasonably well. Their bone structure is just not built to take it and the powerful person knows it. Some people always train with others of the same small stature and never feel a large man's strength. Women who only train with other women in self-defense are certainly doing better than women who don't train but they could also be building a false sense of security by not practicing with men to prepare for differences in size and strength.

Knowing fundamentals of different forms of fighting prepares you for encounters that aren't taught in a style. When you see Aikido people practicing self-defense, they all move like Aikido people. Same with tae kwon do, karate, wing chun, jujitsu, boxing or whatever 'stylist' they are. People who only see 'their version' won't be prepared for something that looks different from what they are used to seeing at their school.

If you want to prepare yourself for what real bad guys on the street may do to you, it doesn't make sense to only practice with a partner who moves like a traditional Japanese karate stylist, in a deep front stance, and 'attacks' with a traditional stepping lunge punch. Have you ever seen anyone move like that outside on the street? You better know how a person with little or no training wings punches at you, because even though it's not a 'good' punch, it could still hurt you.

A wild, unschooled, 'haymaker' may land just because it's goofy and you have never seen such a poorly delivered punch. If all you are used to seeing is 'proper' punching technique, that crazy punch could cause you momentary hesitation, long enough for that one punch to land. Traditional karate, wrestlers, judo, or tae kwon do stylists may not be prepared for a fast jab, cross, hook combination. Boxers may not recognize a basic karate roundhouse to the midsection, or a double leg takedown, simply because they are not used to seeing it. None of these are 'advanced' moves, they are just basics from different systems that work.

KICKS!

There are many pros and cons to kicking for self-defense or sport fights. Advantages of kicking include more power and reach over someone who only strikes with their hands. Since legs are usually about 3-5 times stronger than arms, you can deliver much more power with your feet than is possible with your hands. Your legs are usually longer than an opponent's arms, so good kicking skills can keep someone at a distance and away from you.

Night operations with New York dancer Georgia and her cousin Crissy.

Good kickers can surprise someone not accustomed to kicks. Having the element of surprise, more power and reach over an opponent is a tremendous advantage. All of these advantages mean you could prevail over an opponent with one well-timed, accurate, fast kick.

Bruce Lee's flying sidekick to Kareem Abdul Jabar in the movie **Game of Death**.

Good kickers are usually fairly lean and well-conditioned. Great kickers are usually in exceptional condition. Kicking practice, especially doing high kicks, requires tremendous energy, uses many muscles and keeps your lower body, heart and lungs very fit, so kicking is really healthy for you.

Having all those advantages comes at a price and there are many disadvantages to kicks. If you kick poorly your leg can be grabbed and you can be thrown. You can get kicked underneath in the groin or supporting leg, lose your balance or slip and crack your tail bone or head. You can kick with the incorrect striking surface and hurt your foot or ankle making it tough for you to even stand up, let alone get away.

If you kick slowly and commit your momentum towards your opponent while flailing your arms and leaving an opening, you could run into a counter punch, ending things real quick for you. In a crowd it may be impossible to get your leg up high enough for a groin

JD holds pad for Master Yung Freda demonstrating jumping 'off the wall' roundhouse kick at Grandmaster Ji seminar in Monterey, CA seminar.
Jurg Ziegler

Renee' Timmerman side kicks with Ashley. This is good clean, teen fun.

kick. You could have tight pants on, shoes that are dangerous to kick in or be bundled up against cold weather. The surface you stand on may be uneven or slippery. Many self-defense environments aren't the same as a training facility.

Despite all the disadvantages, it's usually a good idea to develop kicking skills. Even if you don't kick well and have no plans to use kicks for self-protection, you will work up a good sweat practicing, which probably won't hurt you. After a while, you just might be more effective than you thought you could be. Good kickers can deliver heavy power impossible for punchers to deliver with their hands.

Cassandra aka 'KO Lady' roundhouse practice with Master Anderson.

The first time you hold the kicking shield for a man or woman who delivers a good skip in side kick and your feet leave the floor and you get knocked backwards, your Kick Respect Meter goes up 'real high, real fast!' It's much more difficult for opponents to protect themselves if you launch coordinated attacks and hurt them with both hands and feet.

Brianna aka 'Rowdy' demonstrating standing, jump double wide, front kick

After personally dodging and sometimes being unlocated by great kickers who can punch too, watching out for a boxer's hands is almost simple. Exceptions are boxers with hand *and* foot speed (for mobility) that give you problems. A good kicker can cause a great deal of grief to a wrestler or boxer in a self-defense situation, provided the kicker doesn't make mistakes that can be capitalized on.

From a pure **Health and Fitness** stand point, kicking drills are an efficient, mentally stimulating, physical activity that really has no equal in overall lower body development. Kicks don't create large, impressive to look at leg muscles. They develop long smooth, coordinated muscles capable of *delivering brutal power.*

There are countless training methods to work your body to 'be fit.' Kicking drills work most of the muscles below your chest. Even if you only use your self defense kicks to create openings for your hands, effective kicks make you a better fighter.

Joe Lewis and his famous flying sidekick.

I like to say: **"If you want to knock them out with your hands, make them fear your feet."**

Some martial artists don't really understand aerial (jump or flying) kick practice. I have seen those who place far too much emphasis on aerial kicking because they look cool and are impressive. Some of those who focus too much time and energy on high fancy type kicks really believe that, because they can do extremely difficult kicks, any opponent will certainly be doomed if they are so unlucky as to face their flying feet. Maybe, and maybe not.

Undefeated Bill 'Superfoot' Wallace kicked so explosively with his **lead leg**, men like Jem Echollas, who knew what to expect, got whapped in the face without seeing it. Jem has his rear guard up, but simply hasn't reacted. Wallace knew he trained his left foot to go so fast, he could kick Jem's face before he could react and move his hand 8" to defend it.

Plyometric training is very popular with professional 'standard' type fitness trainers. They have you jump back and forth, up and down, and over obstacles. These drills are great! Plain old jumping is extremely taxing to muscles in your legs and cardiovascular system and will suck the wind right out you.

If you are a fighter, your physical conditioning will benefit but your *fighting skills will not be improved*. Yes, regular plyometric training will make you a better fighter than if you didn't jump because you will be in better shape. However, if you want to **do better than that, jump** *and kick*.

You get all the plyometric benefits, **PLUS SKILL DEVELOPMENT.**

Add in the extra muscular exertion from lifting your legs, twisting, turning or spinning to deliver your kick and you will *feel the difference*. Kicks work your abdominal and other torso muscles also. Each time you jump kick a target, you must strike accurately and with the proper striking surface of your foot. It's very important to condition your

That **lead leg** round kick from a different angle. This is **not** a power kick. It is speed, timing and accuracy. Wallace is a wrestler who took the time and energy to learn to use his feet to his advantage. This is **THE HIGHEST LEVEL martial technique, taking them out, from a safe distance, out of their range.**

Todd holds pads 8' high for 6' tall Master Anderson's standing double jump front kick. This training makes a front kick to the solar plexus very easy and develops scary power.

Master Anderson delivers Hapkido 'off the wall' roundhouse kick JD taught him, that was leaned from Grandmaster Ji.

Master Anderson with his 9' jump roundhouse kick. This training makes it very simple to kick a thigh, ribs or neck with Real Knockout Power. If he was just jumping up and down, he wouldn't have the accuracy or technique for lower kicks. Yes, he delivers boxing punches, karate strikes and grapples too.

6 yr old Mika and her flying side kick

weapons for heavy power delivery, which can break your feet if they aren't toughened up.

I have heard those with primitive technical skills talk 'smack' about jump kicks. It's their right to do so and if they want to be fat or strong and uncoordinated, that's their business. There is much more to fighting than jump kicking and while it's unlikely you will be using too many aerial kicks in fighting competition (watch on YouTube how Anthony Pettis uses the same 'off the cage' roundhouse kick to WEC Champion Ben Henderson's head like Master Anderson is pictured doing in the photo to the left) or self defense, there are many benefits to practicing them. It's better if you are younger, full of energy and don't have a bad back, knees or ankles.

Jump kicks are an example of 'Sport Specific' training. Who do you think will be more capable of delivering brutal power in a fight: A kicker or the guy who sprints hooked to a parachute, or jumps up and down, and over things or climbs a Versaclimber?

Practice jump kicks for 'cardio' work, kicking power, accuracy, coordination, control of your body and conditioning of the feet and shins. Does that mean running sprints while hooked to a parachute isn't hard and excellent 'cardio' training? Do I think jumping plyometric style isn't great for you?

No! If you are competing in a Sprint Explosively contest, then sprint while hooked to a parachute. If you plan to enter a jumping contest, practice plyometrics.

Mr. David Massender kicking at JD

If you want to kick someone so hard you break them, mentally and physically, practice kicking and jump kicks. So far, I haven't seen any competitors sprinting or jumping up and down or over things in the Octagon except before the fight.

Since it's important to train wisely, make sure you are landing on a surface with some 'give' to it. Repeated landings on a floor surface that's too hard will cause injuries to your feet, ankles and knees. If you are young, it may not bother you immediately but remember, it's not a Natural Activity to repeatedly jump and land on a hardwood or concrete floor with your bare feet.

Jumping and landing barefoot on a mat, grass or sand will make the muscles in your feet and ankles extra strong and conditioned, provided you do so in a sensible manner, allowing your body time to adapt to the stresses. A regular dose of jump kicking makes you a much better athlete but too much of anything too soon is not good for you and will set your training back due to needless injury.

Be careful and have fun!

Above: My adopted sister 'Feisty' who **gave birth to 6 kids**, leads women's class with her jump front kick. Her kids respect and admire her for her abilities and they usually do what they are told. 'Feisty' will beat me up, if I leave her out of my book. Hi Doc! Miss ya!

Heather aka 'BANZAI'

'Rowdy' with her 'off the wall' Hapkido roundhouse kick, Master Anderson taught her.

The Evolution of Mixed Martial Arts

Ali at his training camp in Deer Lake, PA. His 2nd wife, Belinda, was a 3rd dan black belt in karate.

In 1993 when the Ultimate Fighting Championships made its debut, it was quite a different production than it is today. Thankfully, there are more rules now, and even someone who knows very little about MMA, can tell by watching some of the early fights that the sport has vastly improved.

I remember watching commercials promoting the UFC debut, and eagerly anticipating watching this new form of fighting competition. At the time, I had about 28 years of martial arts training, and wanted to see what this new venue had to offer.

Inoki up kicking Ali

Like most fight fans, I was entertained that night.

Ali taking a leg kick by Antonio Inoki during a mixed art fight in the mid 1970s. This fight didn't go real well. Ali didn't want to go to the mat and Inoki had no intention of standing with Ali. You can see Inoki slapping Loyoto Machida on YouTube to fire him up before a fight.

As mentioned elsewhere, my own mixed martial arts competition experiences were learned by competing for 23 years in wrestling, boxing, black belt karate, black belt judo, and USPSA combat style handgun competitions, so I had an overall perspective of fighting few others had.

Among my first thoughts watching the UFC debut was that the referee was not trained in submissions. Today all the referees jump right in and stop the fight at the first signs of tapping out. I started getting my joints locked, and neck choked, in Japanese jujitsu and judo in 1971 and 1973, and knew how important tapping out was. When you are getting strangled, or joint locked in practice or competition, you want out **now** when you tap! Not in a little while.

Ray Sua kicking a man, who knows to look for these kicks, in the back of the head. Many younger UFC fighters and fans have never witnessed this type of striking skill, and figure if it's not in the UFC it must not work. This is another martial art that has useful things to offer.   Black Belt Magazine

Basketball's Wilt 'The Stilt' Chamberlin proposed a fight with Ali that was talked about but never happened. Wilt is jabbing here with a bent wrist

That first referee stood there watching fighters trying to tap out, looking uncertain and apprehensive at what to do when a fighter was submitting. My thought was that ref was, well not an idiot, but he was untrained, and he had absolutely no business overseeing fighters using submissions. If you watch Big John McCarthy's debut as a referee, he did close to the same thing with the submissions, except not as bad as that first referee.

Big John learned from his experiences, and now is a great referee if he doesn't get over zealous. I have seen Big John tackle the winning fighter off the hapless opponent he's pounding on, and rough up the winner in the process. He's just trying to prevent serious injury to the fella getting thrashed.

For the life of me, I couldn't understand why on earth Royce Gracie's early opponents remained in his guard trying to beat him up. Like many, I had never seen Gracie style jujitsu before that event. That seemed interesting to me; lying on your back with your legs wrapped around your opponent. I knew enough about fighting to know it's rarely a good idea to fight an opponent on their terms.

It seemed nobody fighting in the earlier days was very well rounded in their skills like more fighters are becoming today. The most puzzling thing was guys like Dan Severn or Kimo who remained in Gracie's guard trying to pound him. I just sat there wondering why those guys didn't understand, they shouldn't attempt to beat a man using unfamiliar techniques and tactics by **playing his game.**

Why didn't those guys stand up, move around and punch or kick that submission specialist? Between the referee not stopping fights properly, and fighters not understanding the proper tactics and techniques to beat that type of fighter, I was amazed. It just reaffirmed how many martial artists were still 'stylists.' Those opponents were only doing the best they could with the tools they had. Many early Gracie opponents obviously had not trained outside their comfort zone, with more

Benny 'The Jet' slams another opponent to the mat during an early full contact karate fight.

effective striking work or takedown defense.

I get a chuckle out of Joe Rogan when he excitedly proclaims "Oh! He threw a high kick!" That's funny to me. What's a high kick? Now I like Mr. Rogan, he does a great job, and he clearly is an expert with jiu-jitsu submission terms and tactics. He definitely knows more than I do about Brazilian jiu-jitsu. From my observations, the Gracie style was modified from Japanese judo and is geared towards sport fight contests with rules, as opposed to Japanese jujitsu with it's street or military emphasis.

So, it's a high kick, huh? Mr. Rogan means a high rear leg roundhouse kick, because for most UFC fighters and fans, that's one of the few kicks they know the name of. MMA puts a damper on poor, or mediocre kicking skills. Many of the other kicks I see attempted in the UFC, aren't delivered like a Real Kicker such as Cung Le delivers. Most Real Kickers don't like rolling around on the mat, and know if they are taken down they are doomed, so they stay away from contests where that may happen. Many MMA fighters today are serious about learning boxing. That's much easier to learn than kicks.

Kicks are the most difficult techniques in martial arts to master, *to really be effective with in a fight.* Then you see Gabe Gonzaga kick Mirko Cro Cop in the head so hard, Cro Cop had to have knee surgery. Ahhh! Thats why we want to do all that stretching and kicking!

While watching some kick attempts in the UFC, I notice that, except for a front or roundhouse kick,

Canada's Jean Frenette

Frenette was a karate forms competitor who kicked straight up with a sidekick. I never saw him fight, but he sure could kick in the air. Wrinkles in the photo are Akita caused.

Joe Lewis side kicking Chuck Norris off his feet, in the bare knuckle days before safety equipment. Norris won 3 out of 4 of their fights. Karate fights can take place on a sealed concrete floor, and include groin, and back of the head kicks. Kicking to the head when you are down is also legal.

Black Belt Magazine

the few other types of kicks attempted are many times relatively slow, or delivered with incorrect timing, distance or striking surface. Many of these 'other' kicks are delivered with average ability against well-schooled fighters in great physical condition with quick reactions. This combination makes kicks less effective. To be fair, I have seen some awesomely effective kicks in MMA, probably starting with Pete Williams putting the "Zamboni" (a 'Marvelous' Marvin Hagler term) on the vastly more powerful, Ground and Pounder, Mark Coleman.

Joe Lewis, knocking out an opponent with a karate ridgehand like Machida KO'd Rashad Evans with. Seems Mr. Rogan or other UFC fans, don't know it was a left ridgehand Machida used because they didn't know what to look for. If you doubt this, freeze the frame on a DVD of the fight.

Many of the wrestler types so prevalent in MMA, seldom work their flexibility, and if they do practice kicking skills, they only want to practice the kicks they see in the UFC. They see poor results from mediocre kickers and figure why learn those? It's too much work to kick high, takes too much time, and requires flexibility they aren't willing to invest in attaining.

What's to look forward to in MMA?

If you have been watching the constant change, improvements and more open-mindedness in martial arts and various fighting competitions since the mid 60's as I have, you will have seen many ongoing changes. Years ago in karate competitions, fighters didn't wear any hand or foot protection, and some styles still don't. In the early 1970s, tae kwon do's Jhoon Rhee invented (or marketed) protective safety equipment for the hands and feet, and things rapidly

I have learned that students listen and respond better to someone they can relate too. Submissions have been part of my self defense tools since 1971. George's St. Pierre or Joe Rogan didn't know why Dan Hardy wouldn't tap when GSP had him in an arm bar. Joint lock work for 46 years, allow me to see on TV, that GSP was too deep, and his leverage was more on Hardy's tricep, not on his elbow joint. Someone experienced defending those locks can feel that it hurts, but knows his joint is not in danger. Tough guys can resist improper technique.

changed in favor of more realistic competition.

The PKA or Professional Karate Association started by Joe Corley, allowed karate fighters to hit each other full contact. Those early fights with the Jhoon Rhee safety equipment made it possible to see what strikes really worked. Many early full contact karate fights displayed ample arm flailing, reinforcing the importance of solid boxing skills if your goal was to knock someone out, and not poke out their eyes, or hit their throat, etc.

PKA rules differed from Japanese or Thai kickboxing by not allowing elbow and knee strikes, or kicking to the legs, and required a mandatory number of 8 kicks above the waist per round. These rules were to differentiate it from boxing or Muay Thai, and promote exciting high kicks, making it more appealing to fans. With time the rules evolved and so did the fighters.

My adopted sister, 'Mean' Linda Harris, mother of three, was a brown belt in karate after 7 years training with me. In 1985 she fought in Ed Parker's Internationals in the **Black Belt Instructor Fighting** division. She lost 3-1 in the finals to Linda Denley, the Top Woman Fighter in the world, so I gave my black belt to 'Mean' Linda. She earned it the hard way.

A few men such as Joe Lewis, Bill Wallace, or Benny Urquidez had wrestling and boxing experience, and they also liked to fight 'point,' then 'full contact' karate rules. Some of the early full contact karate organizations had differing rules and use of throws. Things were changing, moving along.

Judo had rule changes making it faster, more exciting and enjoyable for spectators and so did TKD. Other types of fighting contests started showing up. Boxing remained the same, except there were more types of boxing gloves, better mouthpieces, longer boxing trunks, and World Title fights were limited to 12, instead of 15 rounds. This was to prevent needless injury due to exhaustion in the last 3 rounds.

With a big bang, along comes the UFC opening up legal challenges and being referred to by some as "human cock fighting." Today, with all the rules and regulations in place, MMA has surpassed boxing and WWE in pay-per-view sales. The UFC now holds fights in venues around the world, and despite a global economic downturn, has thrived financially.

So what should you expect to see in the years to come? More widespread use of boxing and 'point' karate techniques. Karate techniques! What the!? Yes, karate. Everyone now knows boxing works. For years I wondered how long that would take. Many fights in the UFC today look almost like kickboxing fights with little gloves. The Ground and Pounder days are waning, there will probably always be men who want to fight that way, but those fighters with primitive skills will no longer be able to compete with fighters using mobility like Frankie Edgar, and striking skills like Anderson Silva, who are continually improving.

I was very grateful that Loyoto Machida won a UFC Championship, so that young fighters under the impression that they already know it all, (there's many of those) would consider karate techniques. I know he lost the title to Rua, but I believe that had less to do with styles and techniques, and more to do with Rua being a very tough and determined man. Despite winning a split decision, 'Rampage' Jackson said Machida "Whooped my ass" in UFC 123. Machida grew up learning karate coordinated attacks, which are difficult to deal with if you aren't accustomed to defending against them.

Being raised by a karate teacher father gave Machida an advantage of years of coordinating his hands and feet to work effectively together. He was also exposed to the ground game early, so he wasn't clueless about that aspect like most karate 'stylists' are. Kickboxing techniques combined with seldom seen (by UFC guys) karate blitzes, feints, and different striking techniques, will help keep an opponent wondering what's next. A skilled opponent who delivers rapid, unfamiliar and bewildering hand and feet combinations at you is very confusing. There are many limitations boxing has for self-defense or MMA, but without it's valuable strong points, a fighter is at a serious disadvantage fighting opponents who are skilled in the 'sweet science.'

The same thing goes for 'point' karate. Yes, I know and understand, point karate guys! They don't even _____(you fill in the blank), but if you find top-level fighters to spar with, they will school you in important factors in fighting. Because of the nature of point fighting, power is good, but not as important as quickness, timing, and technical skill. Matches go for a few minutes and a few points, so endurance in an individual match is not a factor; it is in a tournament, but not a single match.

This sport is based on speed, timing, accuracy and technique, so it develops qualities that good fighters need. There's no other sport-fighting contest where 'Bridging the Gap' between you and your opponent is emphasized as much, and therefore, happens so quickly. YES, if all the training you have is point karate, fighting MMA rules, you may be rudely awakened when nobody yells "Stop!" when you get clobbered, allowing you to recuperate. That being said, just like with boxing, we can make use of the good stuff and leave the rest.

Frequent karate type sparring drills, or *light contact sparring* itself, makes you quick and accurate, with good timing. When sparring partners work on footwork, feints, timing, quickness, accurate strikes and aren't pounding the snot out of each other, good things happen. Partners with a mutual agreement to be careful with each other start *opening up and experimenting* with high kicks, or other less basic techniques, because they aren't so afraid of getting plastered if they go too slow, or mess up. More *time* watching, evading, or delivering quick movements, create a technically savvy fighter. In some kick boxing gyms, they pound each other seriously hard in training, making them very tough, but there's a price to pay for that toughness.

Injuries are more frequent and severe, you may find your career shortened, or even suffer worse damage, like Ali or Quarry did. During light contact sparring, it's inevitable that partners will, on occasion, get hit hard by running into techniques while going fast. This type of contact prepares you for fights, but won't *continually beat your brains out while practicing*. Top karate 'point' fighters spar using good…no…*amazing control* of their contact, so they can spar for an hour. Thai style fighters physically can't beat each other as hard as they do for that long on a regular basis, because they are human and will break. If your light contact training regularly includes extended sparring sessions, your eyes get much better at 'quick seeing' and your reaction time drastically improves. People seem to move slower to you because of **time** moving in a sport based on quickness, timing, and technique, **not because of power**.

As previously mentioned, when a fighter practices delivering fun techniques, or experimental combinations because they aren't afraid of getting clobbered, they can really open up and begin developing variety in their striking skills. Variety in your attacks confuses opponents, making them unsure what you are going to hurt them with next. By creating uncertainty and hesitation, opponents are more likely to think about protecting themselves instead of what they are going to do to you. In the future, fighters who train 'sport specifically' with emphasis on fighting mobility, take down defense, kicking skills, karate quickness and deceptive combinations to bridge the gap and of course boxing, are going to excel.

There's a hard road ahead for those like Kimbo Slice or Brock Lesnar who continue to primarily grapple and think of conditioning or 'strength.' Those who 'go do cardio,' or "Hamster Exercises" won't be able to keep up. If a fighter isn't getting their 'cardio' with footwork, kicking and, punching drills, wrestling, or sparring, they are missing the boat. I call exercises *that are great for you,* **but don't sharpen an actual fighting skill or technique,** "Hamster Exercises" because it reminds me of the hamster in the little wheel in his cage, running around inside that wheel, going nowhere. It's *great exercise,* but isn't developing a fighting skill. An example of what happens, is what Anderson Silva did to Forest Griffin who is a seriously tough man, but his training methods are more 'primitive' than Silva's. I like Mr. Griffin, he's fun to watch and listen to.

Technically minded fighters watch how their opponents move, then take them apart. While moving backwards, Silva delivered a perfectly timed, accurate hand speed knockout jab, to a lunging forward Griffin's jaw, which is an example of MARTIAL ARTS, not strength or 'fitness'. MARTIAL ARTS have been evolving for centuries, and are based on technique, speed, timing, and accuracy. Griffin was totally bewildered because he had never experienced anything like that.

This type of striker training will dominate others in the future.

Hughes vs St. Pierre MMA wiki.org

Rousey vs Holm   YouTube.com

Berry vs Beltran pintrest.com

Velasquez vs Dos Santos
MMA-Core.com

Njokuani vs Herodecki
chicagonow.com

pinterest

STRIKING POWER USING TECHNIQUE

JD had the bright idea to lower his guard and bait a high kick, so he could use his wrestling/judo skills to sweep Janesa Kruse to the floor. The sidekick was never seen, just bright colored lights. Herb Steet

Bruce Lee said striking power consisted of *speed, timing* and *accuracy.* I want to break down those components individually and analyze their effects to a fighter delivering a powerful knockout strike.

SPEED - Physics teaches us a LAW regarding how hard something hits: $1/2\ MV^2$ is NOT an opinion, point of view or philosophy. It is a LAW OF PHYSICS. Simply put, if you want to double your striking power, you can double your mass or weight.

The important part of this formula relative to how it applies to a fighter and their striking power, is the Mass times the *Velocity Squared*. For all you non-physics majors out there including myself, I will explain.

Mass in this context represents the weight of the person delivering the strike. Velocity represents the speed of the strike. The *squared* part represents squaring the velocity, which means you *multiply the velocity times itself*, not times 2.

Many people don't really understand this.

JD off the floor, launching a backfist at 'Super' Dan student Janesa. I was paying her back for the sidekick she planted on my face earlier. Even the women students Dan trains are tough. This is a National Guard Armory, and the sign above my head says GET YOUR GUARD UP. Herb Steet

Simply put, it means a person can double their striking power by doubling their weight, providing everything else stays the same. Doubling ones weight is rarely beneficial. If a person practices a technique properly and doubles their speed, they can *quadruple* their striking power. Which makes more sense? Double the weight and double the power or double the speed and hit *four times* as hard? Again that's providing everything else is the same as before. Remember, this is a **LAW of PHYSICS**, not the opinion of a style, system or teacher.

Speed, by itself, is not the total solution. If you punch with amazing speed but miss your target completely, that's no good. If you miss a vulnerable target and hit something hard like their skull or elbow with your bare hand, you will likely be injured. Possessing speed doesn't make you hit your target. If you punch or kick really fast but strike your target with a bent wrist or toes sticking out when they aren't supposed to be, again, it's you who will be hurt. If you are off balance when striking real fast, you may fall down or the results won't be anywhere near the same as if you were balanced.

TIMING
- Good timing is simply striking an opponent as they move into a blow. They could come forward into your straight-line punch, duck downward into your uppercut or move their head to their right and into your left-hook punch.

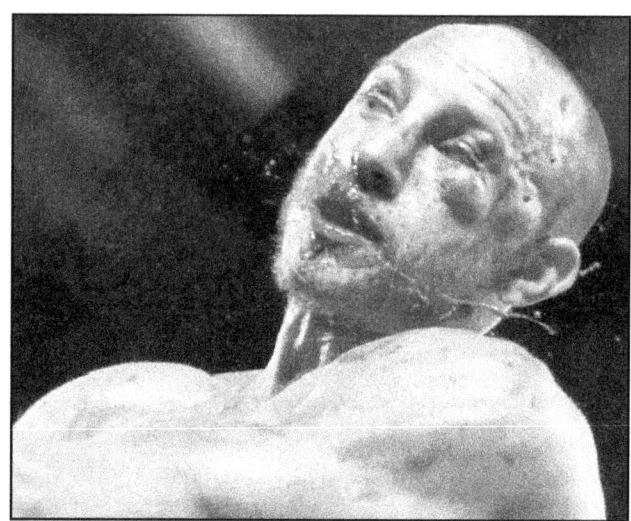

This is an example of what happens when Modern Martial Arts MMA fighter Derek Armstrong delivers a well timed, accurate, jab, with proper form. This is what techniques are about. It's just a jab!   Kim Ventresca 541.761.5729

It doesn't take much movement on their part to be moving into your strike. Them moving into your strike, even if it's only a couple of inches, greatly magnifies the impact. Timing works especially well if you hit a vulnerable spot, a tremendous difference. Experienced technical fighters love catching their opponent rushing in. They are patient, conserve their energy and wait until they have a good clean, accurate shot to a target moving into their strike.

A master technician will borrow the energy the opponent has generated when moving forward and puts that energy on their opponent's own chin or other vulnerable target. The harder and faster the opponent comes in, the harder your strike lands. You don't have to try to hit hard; just keep your balance, deliver a technically correct strike on their vulnerable spot and their own power is delivered to their own weak area.

If you try hard to knock someone out with every punch, you will get tired very quickly. If you let him run into your techniques, you can hurt him without much effort on your part at all. Among the best examples of speed, timing and accuracy I have witnessed is Anderson Silva **knocking out** the very tough and game, Forest Griffin with a *jab* or the powerfully built Kimbo Slice being **knocked out**, also with a *jab* in a few seconds by Seth Petruzelli.

ACCURACY - If you deliver a strike to an opponent and miss or hit him somewhere it doesn't hurt, you waste your energy and expose yourself to a counter strike. If you miss a strike, he can also use your energy by timing a strike against you.

Mr. Bob Barrow (L) and (R) Mr. Chip Wright from Medford, OR with me during 'point' karate tournament days. Chuck Norris trained Barrow, who then trained Wright, who became Norris's stunt double for the Walker Texas Ranger show. Mr. Barrow was a great coach and tournament promoter. These are great guys.

Mr. Wright also became the #1 Nationally Rated Karate Fighter. I will always remember Chip as a very tough guy, with great athletic ability and Supreme Control of his techniques. It's a pleasure to have spent the hours sparring with him. Besides being such a good fighter, he is really funny!

Experienced fighters try to minimize their energy expenditure and exposure to getting hit and hurt, by not wasting their strikes. They capitalize on their opponent's mistakes and let them run into well placed strikes. Technicians borrow their opponent's power and use it against them. Don't just strike somewhere just to strike. Full contact fighters fighting under a set of rules aim for a number of targets depending on the contest and agreed upon rules but the point of their opponents chin or jaw is among the best places to focus a fighter's energy for a knockout.

A near perfect example of the results of deception, proper technique, speed, timing and accuracy is captured in a series of still frames from a film of the Joe Louis - Max Schmeling fight. Even if these photos are over 70 years old, the story is still the same today. If you know how to read them, this series of eight photos tells a long story. Evaluation of this series of photos and understanding the how, why and when of a jab-cross is important and valuable information to anyone wanting to use proper technique to end a fight. Joe Louis is knocked out in this, the first of their 2 fights. In the rematch Joe knocks out Max Schmeling. Joe gets up after this punch but is soon knocked out. These photos offer a great technical lesson of some of the finer points of a very basic 1-2 combination. Let's look in detail at all the things that are really happening in this *instant* of action.

Remember this is just one tiny example of proper technique we can learn from.

PHOTO #1

Max on the right is throwing a distancing, baiting jab to Joe. The purpose of his jab is to insure his distance is correct and to bait Joe into punching at where his head is at that moment but not where it will be in an instant. If Joe punches at Max, he will be moving forward into the straight-line right hand Max is setting him up for.

Max is leaning his body slightly forward in the direction of the referee, part of the deception to get Joe to jab at the wrong spot. This will place Joe where Max wants him, to 'make him miss and make him pay.'

Most of Max's weight is planted solidly on his rear foot, so he can use his powerful leg muscles to push off the floor, which is where power for his right hand punch starts. Max's left foot is positioned to aid in the deception and put most of his weight on his rear leg.

PHOTO #2

While flat footed, Joe has started his left jab towards the spot where Max's head used to be. Max has pushed off against the floor with his right foot and shifted his weight forward and to his left. This places his head inside of Joe's jab, so it will miss. Max has begun retracting his own left jab back to his body so it's out of the way, making room for his right hand to reach its intended target. Max has clearly pushed off his rear leg towards his target and has begun torquing his hips, to let the power generated by his rear leg pushing off the floor, to flow up his leg and through his hips.

Max has also lifted his rear heel up while pushing off, so he can be on the ball of his rear foot at the completion of his punch. Bruce Lee calls this heel up on the rear foot, the **'piston of the fighting machine.'** The rear heel up aids in mobility and is a violation of how traditional karate or tae kwon do rear foot positioning is taught.

Max has shifted much of his weight forward towards his intended target, as can be seen by his lead foot firmly planted now, quite differently than it was in Photo #1. His right hand is now visible on its way to Joe's jaw.

PHOTO #3

Joe's left hand is closer to the spot where Max's head used to be in Photo #1. Joe is flat footed and his right hand is not in bad defensive position but Max's speed won't allow Joe to open his right hand and place it front of his chin, so he can catch, deflect or at least slow down Max's incoming punch.

Max's hips and shoulders have further torqued, and his left hand has been further retracted back to protect his body, getting it out of the way. His left hand could be returning to protect the left side of his face but since Max drops Joe, you can't find too much fault with his technique! Max's rear hand has reached its target but it hasn't followed through past Joe's jaw.

PHOTO #4

BAM! Joe's left jab is right where Max's face used to be, inviting Joe's punch. (See Photo #1.) Unfortunately for Joe, Max made him miss his head and is making him pay. The timing is good for Max; he caught Joe coming directly forward into his straight line, rear hand punch.

Max's hips and shoulders have completed their torquing action. His rear hand and arm are extended and his shoulders have gone past square, unlike how a traditional karate or TKD punch is taught. Max's distance from Joe was just about perfect. Max positioned himself close enough to reach Joe's jaw and have just the right amount of follow through; but far enough away, so his punch builds considerable speed and force.

The power of this punch, started by pushing off the floor with his rear leg, has flowed upward gathering added torque from his hips. This power has flowed from his extended shoulder to his arm and has been delivered to the target by his arm and fist. Max is NOT punching with his arm but has incororated the muscles of much of his body. Max's rear foot is now probably in the classic raised heel, ball of the foot on the floor position. We can't see the whole foot. Max has also shuffle dragged his right foot closer to his left.

In Photo #1, Max's feet were positioned slightly farther from each other, as seen by the distance between his knees in the 1st thru 4th photos. This shuffle drag with the rear foot closes distance and gets Max's weight and momentum moving forward into his punch.

The shuffle drag positions his feet to a better balanced, more mobile position, to either follow up with more punches or evade if needed. Max' weight has clearly shifted forward on his lead foot and his eyes are focused on his target. His punch is very accurate; right on the jaw transferring Max's power directly to Joe's brain stem or whipping Joe's head in a rotational action that causes loss of consciousness.

Max is probably exhaling forcibly out of his nose, keeping his mouth closed to help prevent his own jaw from being broken. This is UNLIKE the mouth wide-open, dynamic karate, tae kwon do photos used by magazines to create excitement. The forceful exhalation adds abdominal muscles to the list of musculature that has been brought into play, in proper sequence, up from the floor (proper technique).

Max's right fist, which should have been relatively loose, relaxed and not tightly clenched (see photos #1 and #2) and should now be solid. His forearm, shoulder and abdominal muscles are probably also very briefly tensed at the moment of impact, creating a solid base and weapon. Excessive tension in any of these muscles before that instant of impact creates a 'braking effect' slowing him down, making his punch less powerful. This relaxation is part of the 'science' of the 'sweet science' (boxing).

A high level of neuromuscular education is required to teach the correct muscles to stay loose while delivering a punch, tense for an instant at impact, then loosening again to ease movement and prevent unnecessary energy expenditure. Unnecessary muscle tension during delivery of a punch also tends to make that punch slightly off target, as well as make you prematurely tired during a full contact situation. This is trying too hard to knock someone out.

I once heard a World Champion boxer after a fight say "Knockouts come by themselves." This means: throw the punch and when they run into it, they get knocked out. You don't have to try for a KO unless the opponent is hurt, backing-up and you want to finish them.

Without the proper tensing of the fist, arm and shoulder muscles at impact, there would be a sloppy 'give' to Max's fist and arm and Joe's jaw wouldn't absorb all the punch's energy. The force generated from Max's leg, hips, back, shoulder and arm muscles are concentrated on Joe's jaw which has moved forward into Max's punch. Again, the faster or harder Joe punches and moves forward, the more it aids Max who is concentrating his energy, as well as Joe's forward energy, onto Joe's jaw.

PHOTO #5

Max's punch has been delivered and he has followed though past his target. Max's weight is leaning forward into his punch, unlike traditional karate punching. The relatively soft boxing glove absorbs energy that a bare fist does not, so a lean in that direction for boxers works well.

Max has shuffled his rear foot farther forward, bringing body weight and momentum towards his target, contributing to his power. Max's right hand and arm are brought up to protect his face while his left is across his body protecting it. His eyes are alert and assessing the damage his punch has done.

Joe's legs are instantly buckling, probably due to the pain stimulus affecting the part of the brain stem called the vestibule spinal tract which maintains extensor muscle tone in the legs. The Reticular Activating System (RAS) is probably also affected. I am light years from being a neurosurgeon but these results seem to be consistent with results I have witnessed from hunting and from Dr. Dennis Tobin's descriptions in the 'Neurologist's View of Stopping Power' from the book **Handgun Stopping Power** by Evan Marshall and Ed Sanow.

Regardless of what is happening from a neurologist's point of view, boxers call the point of the chin 'the button.' They speak of landing a punch 'right on the button.' This works like switching the power button 'off' on an electric machine or toy; it just stops. The side of the jaw also works great as these photos clearly show. Since muscles in the human body receive their messages through the nervous system, it makes sense to attack the 'button' affecting this message delivery system.

Joe's collapsing legs are a perfect example of attacking the nervous system. An additional benefit to this method, is that it usually doesn't require as much effort on your part to accomplish this. Fighters with solid square jaws and big strong necks are usually harder to KO with this method. Strong necks with muscle mass, absorb and disperse some of the shock, so the brain doesn't absorb as much energy but those guys get knocked out too. Strong neck muscles also protect the cervical vertebrae from injury and are very important to serious fighters.

PHOTO #6
Joe's legs have collapsed from under his body; dropping him so fast his jab is still out in the air. Max is still covered up defensively just in case.

It makes a believer out of you when you catch a man just right, using perfect technique, speed, timing and accuracy but aren't trying hard to knock them out and this happens to them.

PHOTO #7
Max has realized his right has landed flush on Joe's jaw, collapsing him 'in his tracks.' His hands are not needed to protect him. In a flash, Max has used deception, speed, timing and accuracy to drop the famous Brown Bomber!

In 2011 Joe Louis still holds the record for Heavyweight Title defenses with 25, over nearly a 12 year period.

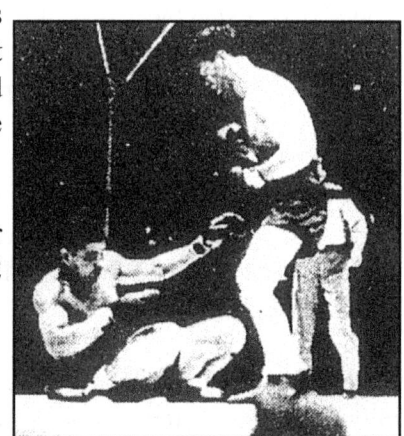

PHOTO #8
Joe wobbles up from this punch, but is pounded out soon after. In the rematch several years later, Max takes a vicious beating from Joe and is KO'd in the 1st round.

AGING AND TRAINING

If a person begins training in the martial arts at an early age, he or she obviously will have a huge advantage over someone who begins developing their martial arts skills later in life. If they train diligently, with good instruction, they will have many advantages over a person with no such training.

I was taught that when someone finally reaches black belt level, *this* was really the beginning of their training. I believe it's important for a young person to train at a sustainable pace if their goal is to train for the rest of their life, which they should do.

This 4 year old on the cover of Sports Illustrated in 1988 is probably quite a martial artist by now if he has continued to train.
Sports Illustrated

Regardless of who they are, everyone needs to pace themselves if they are to 'go the distance' so to speak. As one ages they find changes in their desires and goals involving the martial arts. People may have many reasons to be involved in the martial arts, not all of which involve winning fights. Young people usually give little or no thought to the later stages of life or growing older. If they are lucky they will reach old age, the only alternative to getting old is meeting an early demise. As of this writing, there's nothing one can do to prevent getting older but there's plenty one can do to slow the aging process.

Flexibility work is a very important way to slow the aging process. Most people, even the majority of high school students, are not as flexible as they could or should be. You should strive to continue to stay flexible as you age, as flexibility is a very important, helpful and healthy aspect of an anti-aging lifestyle.

Maintaining good health at any age is very important if you desire to live a happy and fulfilled life. Possessing loads of wealth and material things without the ability to enjoy them, due to poor health and fitness, will not make you really happy.

As you age you usually have less of a desire to get knocked around and bruised than when you were younger. Your body changes and you won't heal as quickly as you once did. You will bruise and at

Getting young kids into the ring or on the mat with their parents to have fun and learn some basics is healthy activity that brings families closer. Exercise and fun can go hand in hand with the proper learning environment.
Bret Blackstone

The Timmerman sisters (L) and 'Bear' Steen when young, and (R) when they are older with JD. You should think of continuing training throughout your life. It's healthier and safer. Katie Timmerman

Nell practicing low self-defense kicking with Master Anderson. She thinks it's fun to practice something new and mentally stimulating with protection skills an added bonus.

Dorothy practicing groin kicks after hip replacement surgery. She has a can-do attitude, and likes knowing more about how to protect herself.

some point break easier.

When I was in my early 20's I was temporarily disabled due to a plantar fascia injury to my feet. I became extremely frustrated because I was unable to stand up and spar so I dug a hole and placed a 4x4 post in the hole with a 5 gallon bucket placed upside down on top of the post to sit on.

I had a cross piece for my feet to hook onto and I adjusted the height of the post so when I was sitting on it my head would be about as high as if I were standing. I loved to get my friends and students to come over and put on the boxing gloves and we would go at it. I was a sitting duck.

I used Bruce Lee's saying to **"turn the stumbling block into a stepping stone"** to improve my hand skills. I couldn't use Ali's "defense is the feet, not the hands" mobility footwork, so I used slipping, rolling with the punches, ducking, parrying, making my reflexes and alertness work for me. Sometimes I got clobbered, and would practice my back falls when I got knocked off the post, but I loved it! Now, after so many years of taking and dishing out punishment, both on and off that post I no longer have a desire to sit on a post and spar.

I sawed off and kept the top of the post to remind me how wonderful it is and how lucky I am just to be able to enjoy the freedom walking around gives me. It's human nature to take things for granted and not appreciate something until it's gone. Martial arts training is meant to help and improve you. Hopefully, you will live to be old and able to help those who are younger learn the things you have learned. If you abuse your body too much when you are young, it may not be much fun when you get older.

The Great Muhammad Ali is such an example; technically, Ali suffers from Parkinson Syndrome, but others believe it is really Joe Frazier, Earnie Shavers, George Foreman, Larry Holmes disease: Too many hard shots to the head toward the end of his career.

Ali's wife, Loni, says Muhammad wouldn't trade what's happened to him for what he has accomplished and doesn't want people to be sorry for him. Ali has always maintained a positive attitude and found a way, some way, any way, to make the best of a bad situation both in and out of the ring. He continues to have that attitude today.

Remember you are human even if you are young and believe you are superman or superwoman. If you subject yourself to unnecessary physical abuse, one day it could catch up to you.

How much is too much? Nobody, including you, knows for sure. Train hard and smart and remember there's a difference between pain and injury. If you do something that makes everyday life painful or impossible then, when you are older, you may look back and wish you had not been quite as reckless with yourself.

'IMAX' Doug Memmott age 70 working the focus pads with retired 'Pistol' Pete. These 'young' men enjoy having fun and the many healthy fitness benefits proper martial arts training provide.

In 1985 'Killer' Lucille Thompson from Danville, IL at age 88, perfoming at the National TKD Championships. If you are too reckless with your body when you are young, it may be impossible to enjoy training when you are her age.

6 year old Mika enjoys flying thru the air with her sidekick. She will be more than most boys will be able to handle when she gets old enough to date. If boys don't respect her, it could get painful!

Lori Massender holding the focus pad for 6 year old daughter Brittani's palm heel strike. This is great family time together.

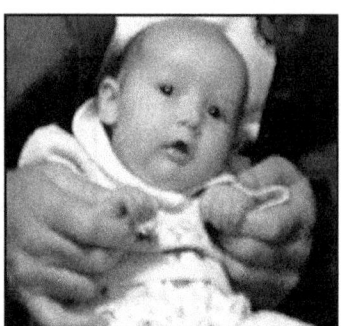
My niece, Bailey Dolmage, learning boxing punches for her first amateur fight.

Well, the fight thing didn't work out like I planned, Bailey opted to be a Princess Ballerina instead :)

Bethany aka 'Sparky' is an example of a young woman who enjoys the workout, and the capability of protecting herself. As I have heard "you can't tell by looking!" JD photo

After a boxing match, with my nephew, Jake, born on my 29th birthday. 'CB' is his Mom. Too many broken noses will make you look funny.

Bill 'Superfoot' Wallace is a man with a body that does unbelieveable things most 20 year olds can only dream of doing. Despite his wrestling base, his flexibility work enables him to do fantastic things. He may look older, but he is still amazing. Century Martial Arts

BREATHING WHEN FIGHTING

Rocky Marciano knocking out Joe Walcott. A punch to the jaw while it's open can lead to injury and unconsciousness. Keep your mouth closed if you are within striking range.

Close up of the impact

It's no secret boxers and kick boxers get hit in the face hard and often. Heavyweight Golden Gloves boxer Tim Howe and Gary Jantzer took me to my first boxing practice in 1968. I was told to listen, follow directions, and keep my mouth closed when punching.

I was told by my first boxing coach to exhale forcefully out my nose when I delivered punches. I listened carefully. I was told to open my mouth, grab my chin with my hand and to push it to the left and right. I did and I believed it when told if I was punched in the jaw with my mouth open, my jaw could be hurt badly or broken.

I was asked if I had seen a human skeleton and if I knew what the little hinge joint looked like that connected the lower jawbone into the rest of the skull. This is called the temporolmandibular joint, a far from sturdy looking thing, fragile almost.

The truth is this*: If you are close enough to strike someone, they are close enough to hit you back* and you don't want to be injured badly by giving them such a vulnerable target as an open mouth. An exception could be if you have a tremendous reach advantage but a good defensive fighter could slip inside and hit you while you are delivering your kick or punch.

If you are giving the mouth wide-open ki yell (called different things in different languages) while delivering your technique, it's possible you can get hurt badly. You see many photos of karate and TKD type stylists punching or kicking, with their mouth wide open. To someone new to fighting, this is *a dynamic, exciting* photo! Stop and think for a minute if you are being instructed to kiai when you punch. Think about that fragile jaw joint and how opening your mouth and putting slight pressure on the side of your jaw with your own hand can cause you some mild discomfort. How can you not envision getting hurt, if you were struck in the jaw with your mouth open? Just think, you too, could be sucking food out of a straw for six weeks like Ali did after the first Norton fight. Having your jaw wired shut doesn't sound like a great thing to me unless you talk too much or need to lose some weight.

Ali in 1973 recovering from the Ken Norton fight.

Who gets hit in the head and face the most? Boxers get hit there a lot more than karate or TKD-type martial artists. Boxers know all about getting hit in the head and face. Boxers can't kick; throw you, claw or do submissions but they do know about getting hit in the face. Did you ever hear Manny Pacquiao, Floyd Mayweather Jr Roy Jones Jr, or Evander Holyfield kiai at their opponents?

Do you think they would kiai if it meant **$30,000,000?** Tyson, Holyfield, Mayweather Jr and De La Hoya have fought for that much money and you can bet they would kiai, if it helped them knock out their opponent. They don't kiai, they keep their mouths shut because they know what happens if they fight with it open. Have you ever seen a photo of a World Champion boxer in a punching exchange or even delivering the KO punch to an opponent who was hurt and in trouble? Did the photo show the Champion with his mouth wide-open 'kiaiing'?

On occasion I have found photos of great boxers in the late rounds of a brutal fight which showed their mouths open. At that moment, the champion was trying to suck in as much air as he could, gasping for breath, not to yell at his opponent. Experienced full contact coaches recognize tired fighters when they see them breathing with their mouths open.

No, I don't think a kiai is useless. I believe a kiai is useful in some self-defense situations where you are not yet fighting but you know you are about to take a beating or worse, if you don't do something. If you know you don't have the option of talking your way out of trouble, running away, playing possum or something, anything else but fighting, you had best strike first.

Ali and Bundini after the Norton fight. Ali said his jaw was broken in the 2nd round, and he fought the powerful Norton 10 more rounds in this condition. Norton says he broke it in the last round.

If you strike with confidence, a loud kiai, proper technique and surprise, the chances are much better you will make it out of a bad situation. If you explode with surprise, they must react to you and your powerful kiai and strike may hurt them so you can escape or convince them you are the wrong person to mess with. If you have multiple opponents and you kiai as you strike the leader, it could surprise and impress the others. If the largest or the leader is suddenly 'neutralized' with sudden authority right off the bat, it makes the others think about the risk of getting themselves hurt. It's also good not to have to worry about the biggest or baddest guy if the others do decide to try to get you.

At the right time (when blows are not yet being exchanged) a powerful kiai has a scary, serious effect. At the wrong time a kiai is an invitation for injury. It's like any other technique. If you throw a right cross when the other guy delivers a sidekick, you may run into the kick and be on the short end of the stick. Same thing with a kiai. When I see photos on the covers of karate, tae kwon do or body building magazines depicting this 'dynamic' facial expression, I know it's to *create excitement* and sell magazines to those who don't know any better. I see such a photo and wonder why they do that. Apparently they just don't know or care about setting a bad example to those learning about fighting. Maybe they are just doing what the photographers want them to do.

Another time it may be good to kiai, is when you have a dangerous opponent hurt and you need to throw 'the kitchen sink' at them so to speak and finish things. You don't want to try that very often. It's easier for them to counter you when you try to hit them with all your power because you are 100% on the offensive and not thinking about defense. My nose was broken boxing because of that. If you believe in the extra power of the kiai (spirit meeting) go for it. Just remember that little jawbone joint, how easy it is to injure and how 'The Greatest' learned his lesson the hard way. How about you, how are you going to learn this important lesson?

While on the subject of breathing, I will mention additional reasons to exhale forcefully when delivering a strike. One is; you tense and help protect your abdominal organs from injury if you are struck there while delivering your technique. When I tell someone I can't hear them breathing as they strike or maybe block and they say "I am, you just can't hear me!" I tell them if I can't hear them, it's not being done correctly. You can hear a good boxer or kick boxer forcing his air out from quite a distance even with other background noise going on. You can tell a real full contact fighter by the way they breathe. Listen to Cain Velasquez breathe when he strikes. That's the way a full contact fighter sounds.

The 'yellers' don't know what REAL FULL CONTACT is about or they wouldn't be exposing themselves to serious injury. When full contact fighters punch or kick and exhale forcefully you can tell what their mental focus is and that they mean business with each technique they deliver. You can tell they are including their mental, physical and spirit power and they are used to getting hit hard. In some styles of karate, fighters do hit each other full contact but don't allow punches to the face. They think that's cheating. I think they are tough but it's unrealistic to expect others who don't know their rules to heed their 'no face punching' rules. Because they aren't used to it, those stylists won't be as prepared for something that's very likely to occur in self defense.

Breathing forcefully with "bad intentions" as Mike Tyson said, helps focus your mental power on the technique you are delivering. You're not thinking about what's for lunch tomorrow or what you did this morning. You're putting the hurt on someone or some thing, even if it's a heavy bag. When you exhale hard, you force much of the air out from the bottom of your lungs, making more room for fresh air when you breathe back in. Shallow breathing doesn't empty much of the stale air, so you don't have as much room for fresh air. Any physical exertion requires good breathing or you get winded real quick.

Your forceful breathing can also help wear down an opponent mentally in the later rounds of a sport fight or maybe even a long street fight. Your opponent could be getting tired also but if you sound like you are fresh and still coming at them with intensity in each shot, it's hard on their psych and morale. They are more likely to think they are tired but you don't sound like you are getting tired and wonder 'Wow, does this guy ever give up!?'

During my years of trying to get people to breathe like a boxer, forcefully out their nose, I have learned that it's hard for some people. It's much easier now because some modern mouthpieces have an airway slit in front so you can clench down on the mouthpiece and still breathe thru your mouth. Men or women who have never played contact sports seem to have a more difficult time with forceful breathing compared to those who have played a sport where they could get the wind knocked out of them. Many women find it difficult to sound like that. I'm guessing it seems un-lady like, forcing air out their clenched mouth but that's OK. Many women can do things I can't.

While watching a TV program about former heavyweight boxer Jerry Quarry, I saw an amazing and unforgettable video segment I wish I could have taped for students to see. That video demonstrates proper breathing in a way no amount of words could express. Mr. Quarry was a top contender for the heavyweight championship in the late 1960's and early 70's. He fought the best including Ali and Frazier. Mr. Quarry has since passed away but the program was filmed not long before his death. Mr. Quarry suffered brain damage from his years in the ring, and was cared for by his brother. He couldn't remember how to spell his name for an autograph. He would get up off the couch and say, "Well, I guess I better get home." His brother would tell him "Jerry, you are home." Jerry would say "Oh, OK" and sit back down on the couch.

It was a sobering lesson for those who may spend too much time getting hit in the fight game. During the program, Jerry was asked a boxing question and he suddenly delivered a combination of punches that looked like he could knock out a mule. His breathing was loud and forcefully exhaled in a manner that gave me goose bumps.

Due to his training, Mr. Quarry's breathing was such a **part of his being,** that despite the fact he sometimes **didn't know where he was or how to spell his nam**e, his breathing while punching technique was awesome. It was done with focus and intensity, and seemed as natural as regular breathing itself. I have never witnessed a situation anything like that before. Jerry Quarry taught me, in a way I had never experienced. I couldn't dream up a better illustration of how **ingrained power breathing is to boxers.**

This is what I teach those who have trouble breathing properly: Breathe forcefully each time you strike during practice and if you ever need to defend yourself, the breath will come out, without thought. Each time a student punches my focus mitts or kicks pads or the shield I'm holding for them, they hear **me** breathe. Each time. If I see a body strike headed my way, it's reflexive action to breath that way, thus helping protect my body from injury.

Jerry Quarry receiving a counter right cross over his jab while fighting Ali. This photo shows that despite having his right foot out of position for a balanced punch, Ali's hand speed, shoulder extension, hip torque, accuracy and timing result in a powerful punch.

Mouthpieces with the airway slit in front offer good protection against the jaw injuries I have been harping about. This a great idea for sport fights because of the additional air breathing in or out as your jaw is clenched down on the mouthpiece. Some kick boxers exhale forcefully out their mouthpiece with an "eeessshhhh" sort of noise forced thru clenched jaws. The actual sound is not important, the forceful exhalation is.

If you want to impress judges at a karate or tae kwon do forms competition, give a real loud yell and growl, with a really mean, scary look on your face.

If you are in a fight, keep your mouth closed unless you want to invite injury.

Natural Behavior

Why watch animals? How can watching them keep me safe?

Animals that get caught and eaten, or who do the catching and eating, behave differently than domesticated animals.

A cow is an example of an animal that's been domesticated by people and has few survival skills. The cow usually has few things to worry about. Watching a cow shows you it's an animal that would be easy to catch. Most cows usually don't think too much about predators because the rancher provides for and protects them.

Pack or herd animals that live together in groups such as deer, monkeys, elephants or apes have developed unwritten social skills and rules they instinctually know or learn as the animal grows up. This allows those animals to live together.

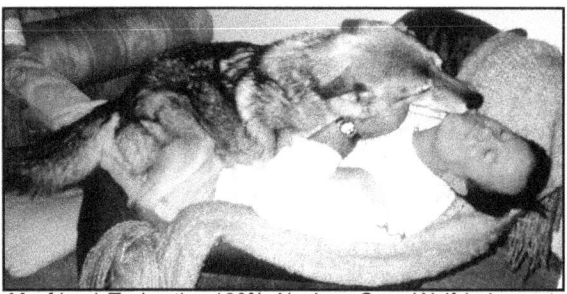

My friend Tasha the 100% Alaskan Gray Wolf belongs to Bret Blackstone. This is really lick defense. Wolves make you quick and aware of your surroundings.   Bret Blackstone

Humans have made many written rules called laws that are for the good of everyone to help make it a safer place for the people to live. Most people depend on the other humans to obey these laws, to keep them safe. The problem for people is when someone else doesn't follow the rules and hurts them. On average, humans have become far less aware of their surroundings because they have grown dependent on other humans to follow the rules. Most humans do follow the rules or laws, so it's natural for some people to get lax about being aware.

Hunted or hunters, large and small, strong or weak, fast or slow, most animals are far more alert and aware of their surroundings than most humans. People are supposed to be too 'civilized' to need to be so aware.

Larry 'The Enforcer' Cook, Kristy's dad, wrestling with this White Tiger for his black belt test. Just kiddin'.' A former Army Ranger, he does this for fun. **Below** This Tiger **does have 'The Enforcer' by the throat**, he doesn't sing as well as his daughter.

Lets say Bill thinks it is 'paranoid' when someone else is aware of what's going on around them. That's fine, Bill may be some human predator's next victim, or Bill may never be a victim in his whole life. Nobody can tell who is next or if something bad will ever happen to a person. What we want, is to make it more difficult for someone to hurt you and by adopting the Natural Behavior of the other animals on earth you are less likely to become a victim.

It doesn't matter how big, strong or tough you are, or if you are an elite member of the Special Forces armed with a deadly weapon. If you aren't alert and aware of what's happening, someone can take your weapon and use it on you. Where ever you go, whichever expert you ask, even if they differ on methods to protect you, all will agree that being alert, aware and avoiding trouble will do the most to keep you safe.

Learn how to stay alert, aware and avoid danger by watching Nature's animals. Like kung fu masters, we too can imitate animal behaviors.

These are behaviors humans used to have, before there were written rules and laws to protect them.

Kristy Lee Cook giving her buddy some love. This family likes Tiger Style Fighting! Being around the Spirit, Power and Quickness of these animals is awe inspiring and unforgettable. If you have ever had a 650 lb. Siberian Tiger do its best to get to you and kill you like I have, (not these tigers) you will no longer think you are quite so tough. In fact, when you are able to think straight again, you will be completely humbled! Just the roar from a Lion or Tiger at arms length vibrates your guts and leaves you with feelings of terror and complete and total insignificance. Check out some of **Kristy's martial arts skills with me on her 'American Idol audition'** on YouTube, or watch her 3rd season TV show **'Most Wanted List'** on the Outdoor Channel.

These Tigers belong to the Amazing Mrs. Ringo who rescues and cares for them in Selma, OR.

Mr. Doug Seus and his Heavyweight 'cage fighter' Bart the Bear. Any takers? Bart is the size of 3 full sized lions. **Vitalground.org**

I like to spend time with Lions and Tigers and Bears, and Akita pups. Except for the Akitas, I'm scared of the full sized ones, I just play with the babies. Even a baby Lion bite on the chin doesn't feel good.

Fluid Motion

'BoSan's' step thru front kick to JD.   Tony Hostetter

Most people know moving with graceful, smooth and relaxed movement is much easier for someone who has performed those moves repetitiously for many years.

The best way to enhance relaxed, fluid martial arts movement is to practice kicking and punching while in the water. Training in the water is a wonderful, time efficient way to train.

Fresh water is about 800 times as dense as air at sea level and weighs about 62 $\frac{1}{2}$ pounds per cubic foot, compared to air weighing about $\frac{1}{12}$ pound per cubic foot.

Water training increases your speed and striking power because your muscles become smoother, more like a swimmers muscles, except you develop the neuromuscular coordination of a fighter. The repetition of throwing thousands of kicks and punches in the fluid medium, not only enhances the development of your fighting neuromuscular pathways, it makes for healthier muscles.

Smooth, flexible muscles receive a better blood flow than bulky, tense muscles. Better blood flow means muscles don't tire as quickly and heal faster because of the oxygen they receive. That increase in blood flow also washes out lactic acid in the muscles which is a result of rigorous training, so pool, lake or river practice is great for recovering.

A pool kick and punch session leaves you tired but feeling loose, smooth and fast. Water resistance makes a 30 minute kicking practice equivalent to a much longer session in the air. If you kick and punch hard in the water, like a boxer or kick boxer does while shadow fighting in a mirror, your cardiovascular system is taxed tremendously. Now this is 'cardio' training for fighters, not 'Hamster Training' as discussed in the Strength chapter.

Pool work, as I call it, is the safest way to kick and punch while recovering from an injury. Water gives a 'massage effect' to your muscles as the water flows over and around them, helping to heal muscular or soft tissue injuries. The sharp, explosive nature of delivering hard punches and kicks is rough on your body. A young person doesn't notice it much, but the older athlete or anyone recovering from soft tissue injuries, muscle strains, pulls, tendon or ligament problems, needs to be careful how they train.

Explosive movements, which are an essential part of fighting, are dangerous to recovering athletes, so slow to moderate kicking or punching in the pool is ideal therapy for fighters. Resuming training after an extended period of inactivity, for whatever the reason, is stressful to the body and pool work provides a safe and effective method for easing back into training. Racehorses that have an injury that prevents them from running are also worked in pools by their trainers.

Everything, including pool work has its disadvantages. Too much exposure to moisture softens a fighters hands and feet, and that's bad for their weapons. Fighters' weapons must be strong and conditioned to withstand all the power their body generates with their techniques or those tools will break.

I broke my right hand hitting my brother, Matt, in the nose on my 12th birthday, so I learned the hard way about having strong conditioned natural weapons. The good part about that broken hand is I learned to write and throw rocks with my left hand.

I read that a young Joe Frazier soaked his face in a salt-water brine to make his skin tougher and less susceptible to cuts, so I guess that's another plus for water.

"You must become shapeless, formless, like water. When you pour water into a cup, it becomes the cup. When you pour water into a bottle it becomes the bottle. When you pour water into a tea pot, it becomes a tea pot. Water can drip and it can crash. Become water my friend."
- Bruce Lee

Spirit Strength

I'm not a teacher of religious beliefs like George Foreman, so I don't go into detail about spiritual ideas. However, I do want to acknowledge those men who believe in their God, and seem able to conquer all others to win a World Title. Many World Champion fighters have given thanks to the God they believe has given them the strength to win.

I have a video of George Foreman after knocking out Michael Moorer to regain the World Title an unbelievable 20 years after losing it. About the time he realizes he has indeed accomplished an 'Impossible Dream,' he looks up to give his thanks, then he goes to his corner to give a brief prayer.

Big George at Rogue Community College in Grants Pass, OR. George used to be a member of the Job Corps there, and credits his experiences there as the start to a good life.
Bob Warren

On HBO, I watched Larry Merchant tell Evander Holyfield "OK enough about the religion, answer the questions about the fight" when Holyfield continued to thank God for his accomplishments in the post fight interview after another of his great victories. I think Holyfield bought his 54,000 sq. foot, $20 Million mansion somewhere about that time.

I heard Muhammad Ali's wife, Loni, say Muhammad gave his autograph freely; and believes each time he gives one; he's doing another good deed helping him get to a good place when

'Smokin' Joe Frazier had Mega Fighting Spirit

his time on earth is over. Many of these men may believe in different versions of God, but it's their belief in a higher power that seems to help them accomplish what they want and get where they want to go. They may have different paths to get there but they wind up on top. It's a belief that works for them; they have been the Champions of the World.

In the Natural World there are animals that exhibit an extra ration of spirit. These animals can tackle other animals many times their size, and physical strength. A great example is the Wolverine. I have seen a video of a wolverine drive a pack of wolves from their kill, take the wolves' dinner and keep it as it's own. The wolverine was out numbered 6 to 1, and each wolf was bigger than the wolverine.

This is a Wolverine! Be on the lookout, Do Not Attempt to pet one!   Duane Scroggins

I saw a video of the same thing happening with a grizzly bear. Grizzly bears are more than 10 times larger, and everyone knows a grizzly bear can be a Very Bad Animal. The video showed the wolverine smelling the kill, following it to the bear, challenging the healthy full size grizzly bear, and driving it away, keeping the food for its own.

How did that happen? I wouldn't believe that if I hadn't seen it. It wasn't its size or strength, but the Wolverine's Spirit that made the difference. The wolves seemed baffled at the wolverine's crazy, wild behavior which made no sense to them. They did their best to keep their kill but the wolverine took it because he wanted it more.

Sister-in-law 'CB' has lots of motherly protection spirit.   Herb Steet

In sports competitions, I learned many years ago that some competitors have a spirit and desire that makes them go farther, faster, longer or harder than the others. That spirit and desire is what makes them work out longer and do extra things when practice is over.

A mother defending her young against a predator will many times drive that attacker away with a display of pure fury and fighting spirit. It's not the physical strength and size that makes a house cat stand up to a much larger dog threatening its young. It's her Spirit.

Some people have what they think is spirit but unfortunately they don't follow thru with the proper training or attitude. Sometimes they cause trouble because they have some fighting spirit but it's often not enough to handle someone who's taken the time to train and be prepared. These excessively spirited but under trained or undisciplined people may get their butts kicked by someone who is prepared and has channeled their spirit into the proper avenue thru martial arts training. Bullies are examples of having plenty of spirit but they lack the proper education, physical training and respect for others. They lack the qualities that good martial arts training teach.

Remember the old saying "It's not the size of the dog in the fight; it's the size of the fight in the dog." That's a truism that applies directly to the SPIRIT. One can cultivate the Spirit in many ways. The way you choose is up to you. I'm not suggesting how or which you should follow; there are many other people who will suggest that to you. The Champions listed below have their ways and it has worked for them.

Except for Genghis Khan, the worlds greatest conqueror, who prayed to his God Tengri, and Geronimo who prayed to Yusun, I have heard all these World Champions listed below, and many others, thank God for their accomplishments.

Below is an elite group of men that must have something going for them... I'm just sayin.'

Partial List

Genghis Khan – Tengri
Geronimo – Yuson
Muhammad Ali
George Foreman
Archie Moore
Manny Pacquiao
Anderson Silva
Cung Le
Roy Jones Jr
Benny 'The Jet' Urquidez
Randy Couture
'Sugar' Ray Leonard
BJ Penn
Georges St. Pierre
Wanderlei Silva
Matt Hughes
Evander Holyfield
Floyd Mayweather Jr
Floyd Patterson

George Foreman earned $100 Million in the boxing ring, and more than $300 Million selling his Grill.

STRIKERS DEVELOPING BOTH SIDES

Most people know that boxing and kick boxing competitors have a more realistic feeling of fighting than tae kwon do (TKD) or 'point' karate competitors. However, both TKD and 'point' tournaments are valuable learning environments.

TKD and point fighters learn and are excellent at things full contact fighters aren't, but that's another story. If you want to compete and excel in MMA or striking competition like karate, boxing or kick boxing, here are some good ideas.

Both sides should be developed, enabling you to lead with either side forward. In boxing the traditionally accepted method is to place your dominant hand to the rear. Since most people are right handed most boxers are left lead. Boxers who lead with their right, are mainly left handed people such as Manny Pacquiao.

Many experienced martial artists know Bruce Lee advocated a strong or dominant side forward fighting stance. Since there's a different attitude, preparation, set of ethics and rule system in sport fighting contests than in self preservation, the development of both leads may be more applicable for fights in the ring. Regardless, it still makes good sense for self defense situations. If you receive an injury in a self-defense fight, you may need to make adaptations or an opponent may be open for techniques delivered with your other lead.

'Super' Dan's 'Geronimo Face' during karate fight with JD. Dan is a striking Grandmaster whose technical ability and speed is amazing and inspirational. I watched this 145 lb. skinny guy tear up Hvy Wt. Rich Mainetti for a Grand Championship.

At one point, Rich threw a high roundhouse kick and Dan countered as if he already knew Rich's move, dropping to the floor and delivered a perfect sidekick up to Rich's groin (like the photo below) briefly lifting Rich off his feet. That's legal in this sport.

Since boxing is time tested and not based on theory, when someone gets knocked out it's due to a punch or a series of punches, so we can assume those boxing punches really do work! Boxing defense is also time tested. The way a boxer uses defensive movements, chin tucked and protected, footwork, slips, parries, bobbing, weaving, rolling with the punch, etc. These all work to help prevent a boxer from getting hurt.

If a fighter has an open, progressive mind and uses the

Brother Richard Dolmage with dropping counter sidekick to JD   Herb Steet

(L) 6'7" 250lb Devin 'The Destroyer' Tandy, trained in traditional boxing for 5 years with Jack, and his son 'Sugar' Shane Mosley. Devin opened his mind, got out of his comfort zone and learned to use both leads, grapple and even kick, to fight MMA. Devin delivers straight left to 'Captain' Chad Staten.

'The Destroyer' out of his comfort zone for a boxer.

'Captain' Chad with his 2 MMA Title Belts

time tested techniques, plus adds modern concepts to the time tested program, he or she can be a step ahead of the competition.

There have been many times I have advocated developing a boxers other side to lead with. It's much the same resistance to change that a traditional martial arts stylist has. Boxers usually feel uncomfortable in a stance they haven't worked or practiced in, and they don't like it. When a boxer accustomed to usually watching left lead fighters, faces a right lead boxer, it makes him less comfortable. Most boxers don't spend as much time watching 'southpaws' delivering punches at them.

If boxers are not as used to watching and dealing with punches from the right lead, then they can't be as experienced dealing with those punches. That's providing they don't have a left handed primary sparring partner. This is a general observation rule and of course there are exceptions to every rule. If a boxer delivers a punch properly, his body should be generating most of the power. His arm just delivers that body generated power, so why shouldn't a rear hand punch be just as powerful delivered with the other arm?

World boxing Champ 'Marvelous' Marvin Hagler used to switch leads and confuse opponents by giving them a certain look for a while, then switch. Next thing Hagler's opponents knew, he was pounding them from the opposite side. It only takes a split second to slip in a good shot and stun them, then follow up while they are hurt. The capability to create momentarily hesitation or confusion in opponents, is very beneficial.

I remember working with a boxing trainer; a good guy named Tony, who was training Joe Hipp for a WBA World Heavyweight Title fight in 1995. During a workout, Tony was holding the focus mitts for me to punch. I was punching away just fine with my left side forward. As always, I stepped back with my left foot to punch right side forward and Tony asks me what I am doing. I said "I'm switching sides." He said "Don't do that, it confuses me" as he was holding the mitts.

I started laughing. I had told so many boxers it confused their opponents when they switched sides, and now I was confusing a boxing trainer who was only trying to hold the focus pads for me. I found that very amusing. It must be confusing if a boxing trainer, preparing his boxer for the WBA Heavyweight Championship of the World and he's confused just holding focus mitts for someone punching with a right lead.

Former top 10 rated heavyweight Joe Hipp and his trainer Tony, working the focus mitts for his WBA World Title Fight. Lloyd C. Davis

At the time, Mike Tyson was returning to the ring following his release from prison by fighting Peter McNeely on the undercard of the Bruce Seldon - Joe Hipp Title fight, in which Hipp was stopped in the 10th round.

Many coaches or instructors don't feel comfortable with something they don't know much about or can't do. In their mind, if a boxing coach can't punch with authority with either side forward it must not be a good thing. They didn't learn how to do it, they don't know the advantages and they make up reasons why you shouldn't do it. It's

JD showing Hipp some upper body gymnastics stretches for relaxed, and fluid punches. Lloyd C. Davis

the same thing with many other martial arts schools. If a karate, TKD or jujitsu instructor can't box they sometimes say negative things about boxing. Sure boxing has it's disadvantages.

There's nothing wrong with being versatile and able to do things others can't. Be versatile, confusing, hard to figure out. Develop fighting skills with either side leading so you hit harder and with more deception. Punch like those who won't learn to lead with their other side aren't able to. You will find that as time goes on, by practicing punches with either lead, you will be able to do some things on the opposite side better than your regular lead.

I will assume that your right hand is dominant, so your right jab will be a slightly heavier punch than your left jab. Generally, the dominant hand is more muscular and slightly slower but stronger when it lands. The strong side lead is very effective against an aggressive fighter moving forward into your very stiff jab, helping to keep them off you. The faster left jab seems to work well as an offensive weapon because of it's effectiveness against a distant opponent who you are trying to reach quickly, without getting hit.

You don't want to be slow when being offensive because you may be the one running into the counter punches! I don't want to say that you should only be defensive with the right jab and offensive with the left jab. That's silly. It's just something to keep in mind.

JD delivers left cross to bag with 'Thor' support

Practice leading with either side and see what works for you but don't just quit leading with your other side because you feel awkward. Remember how at first it wasn't easy to learn many things with your regular lead. A straight rear hand lead punch, such as a boxing straight right lead, is dangerous to throw because it can take longer to deliver that rear hand lead. Since it's dangerous, it's not used much unless the fighter delivering it feels confident in his speed and power.

It's a very effective punch if done correctly and with great quickness. If you lead with your strong side, presumably your right, your lead straight left seems quicker than the right straight lead. I have used this rear lead very effectively in boxing because it's unexpected. If you are fast, you can capitalize on the fact your opponent probably doesn't see it much in practice and it also gives you a longer reach than your lead jab.

If you place your feet in a right lead boxing stance and jab without pushing off your left rear foot, or stepping forward with your right lead foot, your jab will reach a certain distance. Have a partner hold up their hand at the distance your jab reaches, then jab slowly and lightly at their palm, just to establish your maximum jabbing distance without leaning or stepping forward.

Now deliver a rear straight left punch straight to the target without strength or power, just push off with your left rear foot up to the ball of your rear foot, and twist your hips to the right and extended your left shoulder. Your left hand should be about 6 inches past where your lead right jab went. The rear foot push, twist of the hips and reach and extension of your left shoulder give you the distance. You haven't taken a step, yet your rear hand reaches farther than your lead hand.

Make certain you have some width to your stance when you punch with your rear hand, so you maintain your balance. Remember, if you aren't *real quick* delivering this punch, you could be running face first into one of their punches. If you push off hard with the rear foot in the direction of the target and reach out past your balance point, you could fall forward on your face unless you take a step forward with your left foot to regain your balance. Your left foot will now be your lead foot. If your opponent is far away, you can reach him unexpectedly with that straight left punch, because you really reach out there if you know you can regain your balance by stepping forward.

You can set this punch up by distancing your opponent with that lead jab. By not stepping forward when you deliver your lead jab, you can give him a false sense of your effective range. You can lull him into feeling safe, just a little too far away from you to reach him with that lead jab. You can get him into a slightly less alert mode if he thinks you can't reach him with your jab.

When you sense the time to fire, explode that straight rear punch and regain your balance by stepping forward with your rear foot if you have to and just continue punching without missing a beat due to a stance change. You can cover a great deal of distance and surprise him this way.

Leading with either side forward has many advantages. Take the time to develop both.

Multi-time International Black Belt Karate Champ and striking GrandMaster 'SUPER' DAN SAYS SO!

'Super' Dan teaching JD about karate 'bridging the gap.' The quickness, timing, and accuracy of this sport has a very important place in MMA. Despite being stronger than Dan, it did me little good if he was too quick and technically savvy. This grappler/boxer had to learn, adapt, and train differently for a quicker, more confusing sport. Herb Steet

'Super' Dan with his International Finalist student 'Mr. Bill' Rooklidge. JD received a great deal of help from these two men and is very thankful to them.

TRADITIONAL VALUES

Grandmaster Ji, with Bruce Lee in Lee's final movie **Game of Death**, teaches proper values to students along with diverse and practical fighting skills.

MARTIAL ARTS used to teach good character values. These values are definitely still taught by some but more recently some of these core values seem to have eroded away and been forgotten, by some of the new nontraditional mixed martial arts gyms. Older more traditional martial arts systems generally emphasized a higher degree of character development.

Generally speaking, todays younger men and women interested in mixed martial arts are being taught excellent physical fighting skills from various styles but often the important core values are being omitted. It's not right to state that you can't find character development from mixed style instruction today but that important part of MARTIAL ARTS seems harder to find.

JD respects Steve Dietz as he delivers a close sidekick in the late 1970s. Mr. Dietz is the powerful man JD is jump kicking, on the cover of this book.

Grant Kirby

An example of this is listening to the UFC's Dana White talk in interviews or on the Ultimate Fighter TV show. I am very thankful and appreciative for all Mr. White has done to promote, improve and provide exciting MMA fights but he doesn't sound like a role model for youth. In my opinion, his foul mouth is not a good example to young people. I'm far from perfect, I cuss too sometimes but I try to be aware of who's listening before I use bad language.

Mr. White is very financially successful however, so he doesn't care what I think. I wish the UFC would learn to emulate the even *more financially successful* NFL, NBA, or MLB. They would **never ever** allow one of their representatives to speak publicly with language Mr. White uses. This hurts some mainstream acceptance to this violent sport that I care about. Watching bonehead activity such as drunken door smashing or peeing in a

Proper training attitudes develop trust and respect for your partners. Brother Richard Dolmage delivers a groin kick to JD. Respect for others should be carried to others you deal with in daily life.
Herb Steet

housemates bed on the Ultimate Fighter TV Show, are not really what Martial Arts are about. Apparently young people watching think that's cool. I'm wondering if those who think that's cool, want to be treated that way or have their kids act like that at their house?

More recently on the show coach Georges St. Pierre taught his team to be nice to people. GSP has a traditional martial arts background so he's been exposed to more character development than the standard MMA boxing/wrestling gym offers.

I believe GSP is among the ***very best examples for youth to emulate***. GSP conducts himself like a gentleman both in and out of the Octagon. Some may interpret that as weakness until they get their big mouth shut like Josh Koscheck did in UFC 124. With True Ambassador Like Class, after schooling Koscheck, GSP was respectful and gracious to his opponent unlike the way Koscheck treated him before their fight. Josh changed his tune afterward, a good ass kicking has a tendency to do that.

Before commercialization in the martial arts things were much different. I'm not saying commercialization has been bad, it has made it possible for many more students to find and enjoy some form of martial arts training.

Years ago many martial styles were much more harsh and difficult. Only very tough, devoted individuals were physically capable of withstanding such abuse. Masters adopted a frugal, harsh lifestyle and didn't enjoy many pleasures of life outside the arts they loved. A long time ago some masters made it very difficult for interested students to receive their knowledge. There are still a few masters like that. A student wanting to learn from the master had to prove their deep sincerity. It may have taken six months of reporting to the master and standing in a horse stance for an hour, then going home, to prove his worthiness.

Masters were reluctant to devote their time and energy to a new disciple who wasn't 100% committed and capable of his physical, mental and spiritual demands. Few people today would pay for and tolerate six months of standing around in a horse stance. I'm not saying that's the best way to learn to fight. Personally I have zero interest in standing stationary in a horse stance. I wouldn't stand that way in a fight and don't train that way even if it is great for the legs. If you want to learn a particular art that requires you to stand that way for extended periods, that's your business.

Respect and courtesy in daily life, personal integrity and honesty, are examples of the important character qualities a good martial artist should strive to live by. Just because you train to be able to defeat someone in a fight shouldn't mean you want to fight in the street. If you train hard at your school or gym you should channel that fighting spirit in a positive direction. If you really love to fight, great! Enter various sport fighting competitions with rules, sportsmanship and learning opportunities. Competitions allow you to meet others, make friends and learn from people outside your area.

Remember sport-fighting contests in various forms are not real fights but they definitely help prepare you to protect yourself and those you love. You just need to know the limitations of sport fighting contests and not believe you are invincible because you are the Champ of the contests.

James Dolmage and his protege' Master Irving Anderson

Respect, courtesy, consideration of others, hard work ethics, positive attitudes.

As Bruce Lee said regarding students who compete in competitions but want to be ready for self protection,

"Know the rules, abide by the rules, dissolve the rules."

Mixed Martial Arts: Before jujitsu, karate, kung fu, tae kwon do, Thai boxing, judo and full contact karate matches, the competitors bow to the referee then bow to each other before they fight. This respectful action is omitted for some reason from MMA fights and I believe it should be included. **Above** Jem Echollas and Bill Wallace bow with Jim Harrison as referee.

Lack of respect for others and their property is a major problem in todays society and it makes others angry and sometimes violent.

Dealing with respectful, courteous people sure makes the day go smoother. I have included in this book creeds from Chuck Norris and Ed Parker, which their students were required to memorize and practice in their daily life. There are many more creeds and rules from other Instructors but if you follow these you will certainly be off to a great start. Remember *'what goes around, comes around.'*

I try to be fair, so I will say that in the October 2010 UFC magazine, and other magazines, Mr. Dana White seems to have either matured or realized the things I said above about him made good business sense. His interview is very professional, upstanding and respectful.

I'm sure this positive example will only help the acceptance of MMA by those sensitive types who think it's a horrible, barbaric sport watched by heathens. Then they may sign up for UFC Pay Per View! I too share his belief that one day MMA will be the Worlds Biggest Sport.

Since this was first written Mr. White seems to have gotten the message. I haven't heard every word he has spoken but he seems much more aware of his language when talking to the media and it shows. I use bad words too but try not to use those words when I shouldn't.
The UFC has been sold for $4 Billion and we will see what that means to the fighters and us fight fans.

Thank you Sir!

Forms and KATA

'BoSan' and her own personal artistic version of her form.

Since there are still people practicing forms or katas, and probably always will be, I'm including this chapter. I have practiced forms and won a few black belt karate forms competitions. I teach forms to those who want to learn them, for whatever reasons they may have.

I help them create their own unique form to fit their individual personal expression. I give them ideas and help them with the choreography to make it flow and 'look right' to the judges. A good kata or free style form is, as Ed Parker described it, an excellent way to display your "encyclopedia of techniques." You can display your 'art,' and physical abilities to others in a manner that doesn't require a partner.

A freestyle musical form with many kicks, athletic and sometimes acrobatic type moves, done with intensity and power by a skilled practitioner, is entertaining for me to watch, as long as the performer remembers it's supposed to be about a self defense fight. Some of the modern forms are more gymnastic in appearance and quite a distance from something resembling fights.

I'm not sure why some performers deliver kicks with improper striking surfaces of their feet in these freestyle musical events. If they hit someone their toes would break.

Pam as an 11-year-old forms competitor. Many young ladies are not very interested in getting hit at this, or any age. This activity definitely improves young peoples' health, confidence, coordination, balance, and ability to protect themselves.

Pam 22 years later, 7 months pregnant with her 3rd child. Pam has a 'can do' attitude and is much better able to protect her children than most mothers.

Kicking that way makes no sense for an art form based on defending oneself. I really don't get that.

I enjoy musical forms. They can draw new people to the martial arts because of the beauty, grace, power, and athletic ability that's displayed. Form practice to good music can be a superlative way to improve your aerobic fitness, develop many of your kicks and some of your hand techniques. Since you have a set, definite goal when working on your form, you can usually feel and see improvement at the end of a practice session.

Sometimes it's harder to see daily measurable improvements in other types of martial arts practice. This measurable improvement of things coming together for you can be mentally rewarding and give your spirit a boost.

When I practiced for forms competition, it was usually because I was recovering from an injury of some type preventing me from black belt karate fighting, but I could still train. I remember getting extremely winded if I performed my form several times without a rest. My personal forms included many high and jump kicks and other physically demanding moves. I practiced hard and was surprised at the degree of stress I placed on my cardiovascular system.

I know how great kicking is for a person so, I believe forms have many positive benefits, if the forms practiced are intense. I learned something about forms competition that I couldn't have learned any other way, except from actual experience. While performing a form in the finals of a karate tournament, you are the only one everyone is watching. When fighting, your focus is on your opponent. The crowd is out there in the background.

Timber aka 'Little Fox' and a self defense sidekick during her form/dance performance during a beauty pageant.

If you make a big mistake in the Finals, everyone sees you because you are the only one to watch. That pressure or stress is good and helps you in many ways. Life puts you in stressful situations and learning to deal with pressure while maintaining your cool from this type of experience, is very valuable. It's great for helping people develop confidence in their everyday lives.

An area I would like to address here, is that there are teachers who insist you must learn forms to be able to fight well. If you haven't read Bruce Lee's book 'THE TAO OF JEET KUNE DO,' you probably don't know he refers to prearranged kata or forms as "vertical death."

If you enjoy practicing and performing forms, that's fine. Who am I, or anyone else to say you shouldn't? I did forms competition and I teach forms. If you enjoy learning the tradition behind a particular style and want to learn how they fought long ago and far away, why shouldn't you? A positive minded martial artist should allow others to practice martial arts to the degree of interest and ability they are capable of.

Criticizing someone who doesn't want to, or can't fight MMA or Muay Thai matches, is not in the true spirit of the martial arts.

Respect and admire those who are trying to do the best they can with what they have to work with. Remember the true spirit of martial arts is to try, improve and do the

'BoSan's' roundhouse kick while competing with her form 'Bushi No Nasake.'
Linda Harris

best you can. There are many able bodied people who don't try; they just sit and watch. In my book, anyone who gets out and tries, is doing much better than those Sitters and Watchers who seem to be full of advice for others.

Give encouragement to those who have lost a match or performance. At least they got out there, unlike those big mouth bozo's in the crowd who boo competitors. I wish there were a seat ejection button I could press when I hear loud mouths in the crowd boo a competitor just for being there. Sorry, that really fries me! Show some class and respect!

If you are being instructed to memorize many movements in a set, prearranged order and the moves must be performed 'just so' for you to be able to fight effectively, then someone's telling you a crock of hooey. Of course there are body mechanics to master, but if your hand or other body part is supposed to be positioned exactly in a certain way, in a postured stance, well... fights just don't work that way.

Fights have no predetermined order, period. Why on earth would you need to memorize many moves in a prearranged order? Even if all the movements and techniques practiced in your form were practical for fighting in the 21st century, why take the time and energy to memorize the order? Why make everyone learn the same thing?
Because of tradition, following someone's idea of how things should be done in their 'style.' OK fine, if that's what you want to do for whatever reason, you have that right. Just remember fights are spontaneous and NEVER follow a pattern, any pattern, whatsoever.

Stevie Nicks of Fleetwood Mac and her instructor Bob Jones.   Black Belt Magazine

Except for beginners learning the fundamentals, making everyone memorize the same forms to pass a test for promotion, seems egotistical to me. In the very early stages, keeping it simple and the same for everyone makes good sense. They don't have the knowledge yet to be creative.

I enjoy watching a group of men and women all doing the same form together in synchronization, in a demonstration of the martial 'art' of their style; however, it doesn't seem to be an example of development of individual capabilities. If everyone on the demo team wants to be there doing the same form for a demonstration or competition, thats great! My opinion is, why make everyone in class do the same thing to be promoted?

To me, it's as if a teacher, or the founder of the style is forcing their will upon many others. Remember, there are many different and opposing ideas on the subject of fighting. That's why there's so many martial arts 'styles.'

There are many 'Stylists' with a limited knowledge of other methods of fighting outside of their particular 'style.' These 'stylists' can be very enthusiastic about the importance of learning 'their' forms.

Many times I have seen the 'Big Importance' placed on learning their forms, because that's all the teacher knows. They can't teach something else that's effective

because they don't know something else. When they began learning, they were taught their 'style' is the all-important best method and the masters of long ago and far away used to fight to the death using these moves.

These kinds of teachers bought into that story when they were first learning and continued to devotedly learn that 'styles' methods. As a result, now as teachers, they need to keep students paying their dues by teaching these forms to their students.

There is absolute truth to the saying that you will react under stress the way you have been trained. If your goal is to learn to defend yourself, why not train to react spontaneously with 21st Century movements and techniques? If self defense is not your priority, and you enjoy the 'Art' of a style, that's a whole different story.

Karen Sheperd
I first saw Karen perform in 1979. She did a kung fu broadsword form in the dark to a strobe light while dressed in a white silk outfit. Karen is a former International Forms Champion, movie star, and fitness instructor.
karatediva.com

A limit of 3-6 moves in some preset order is about the limit of practicality. This is a good number of moves for a combination, then things will be different. What will the effects be on your opponent be after that? An opponent should have some reaction to your first strike. How many of those techniques landed? What were the effects? Are you still on your feet or are you on the ground? The options and variables to what can happen are endless.

Police officers have reacted in gun fights the same way they were trained to do things on the practice range. Some died because of poor training while others survived because of realistic practice for a life or death situation. There are documented accounts of police officers in the past who were trained on the practice range to reload their revolver by emptying their spent cartridge cases into their hand, then put the empty cases in their pocket to be saved for future reloading.

The Karate Diva in Action!

They were then trained to grab their speed loader from their belt, shove fresh rounds into the empty cylinder, close it, and resume firing. Some officers have died in gun fights with empty cartridge cases in their pockets, and their speed loaders in their hands. They had taken the few extra seconds to save the empty cases instead of just opening the cylinders, dumping the cases on the ground, reloading, and returning fire.

Common sense would tell a reasonable person to skip that extra 'save the empty cases step' in a real gun fight and just dump the empties. Under stress people react as they have been trained. This is just a single example and while extreme, is true. You probably don't want to do something reflexively for the tradition of your style; that's no longer practical for modern self defense if someone tries to kill you.

Do tournament wrestlers, boxers, kick boxers, judo competitors, UFC or other MMA fighters train to fight by remembering a preset series of moves? Nope. Memorizing moves makes no sense when fighting another human. Those fighters are only interested in beating opponents without getting hurt. They don't care about style, tradition, 'mental' or 'spiritual'

practice or other reasoning to practice prearranged, out dated moves used by masters of long ago and far away.

If you like forms, great, keep practicing them for all the positive reasons I mentioned earlier. Don't make the serious mistake of assuming you're real tough just because you know some good forms, and don't believe you have to learn forms to be a good fighter.

International and World
Karate Fighting Champion 'Super' Dan Anderson

SAMURAI WARRIORS *who trained to fight to the death, would also practice flower arranging, bonsai, calligraphy or playing a musical instrument to maintain balance in their lives. Forms practice will also help maintain such balance.*

Ji, Han Jae
Biography

Ji and Lee fight in **Game of Death**.

Ji teaches many extremely painful Hapkido techniques. Prior to training with Ji, JD believed these arts were of limited value thinking "How are you going to grab 'Sugar' Ray Leonards hand when he's punching at you and apply a wrist lock? Well, I learned that not everyone punches like 'Sugar' Ray, and if you practice these techniques, and use them at the correct time, they hurt REALLY BAD! I'm now a believer! Master Yung Freda is feeling the pain here. Jurg Ziegler

When writing a Korean person's name in Korea, their last name goes first, then their middle name, followed by their first name. Ji, Han Jae was born in 1936 in Andong, South Korea. At the age of 13 he began his physical training with Choi, Young Sul, learning Japanese yawara for about 5 years. Ji is considered to be Choi's top student.

Ji began his mental training at the age of 18 under a man known to Ji as Taoist Lee. Taoist Lee trained Ji in the use of the bo (6' stick), the short stick, Korean Tae Kyon kicking methods, and meditation. A woman monk known to Ji as 'Grandma' taught him spiritual techniques for almost 5 years.

In Andong, at the age of 23, Ji opened his first dojang (school) and was the first to use the term 'Hapkido.' Ten months later, Ji moved his dojang to Seoul where approximately 75% of the nation's population lived. In about 1958, Bong Soo Han of the **Billy Jack** movies began training under Ji and continued to do so until the late 1960s when Han moved to the United States.

Master Han and Master Myung Kwan Sik, who is the president of the World Hapkido Association, began training under Ji at approximately the same time and Ji, Han Jae, promoted them to 9th Dan in 1984 and 1986 respectively. In 1962, Ji began his job as bodyguard to Korean President Park who had him working in the Korean Presidential quarters, the Blue House, for 18 years. Ji became politically well connected in this job and was in a position of influence.

While in Korea, Ji was also Chief martial arts trainer for the 300 Secret Service bodyguards protecting President Park. In addition Ji trained the Korean Police and Military academies as well as the Korean Special Forces.

In 1969, the United States Pentagon had an information exchange program with the Korean Government, and Ji visited the United States to train some of President Nixon's Secret Service bodyguards, FBI agents and Office of Special Investigation personnel. During this exchange program, Jhoon Rhee introduced Ji to Bruce Lee, who was very impressed with the knowledge and abilities Ji demonstrated, and asked Ji to teach him.

Above These are photos of Grandmaster Ji teaching a black belt seminar at the First Annual Great Karate Summit in New York in the early 90's hosted by George Tan. JD arranged and assisted teaching the seminar for Ji. Mr. Tan provided us with the photos of Ji and Lee from **Game of Death**. There are many unique ideas, concepts, kicks, and techniques shared by Ji. JD photos

In the early 1970s, Mr. Wong from Golden Harvest Film Company hired Ji as an actor, fight choreographer, technical advisor, and trainer for marital arts movie stars.

Bruce Lee had Grand Master Ji wear a GOLDEN BELT to represent the "Highest level of martial artist" when they fought in Lee's final movie Game of Death.

GM Ji demonstrating a basic Hapkido knee strike to John Beluschak of Pittsburgh. I had a little room and wanted to include the former pro wrestler 'Johnny Sweat'. In addition to being a real strong tough guy, he REALLY makes me laugh!
Jurg Ziegler

ED PARKER

CREED

"I COME TO YOU WITH ONLY KARATE, EMPTY HANDS. I HAVE NO WEAPONS, BUT SHOULD I BE FORCED TO DEFEND MYSELF, MY PRINCIPLES OR MY HONOR, SHOULD IT BE A MATTER OF LIFE OR DEATH, OF RIGHT OR WRONG; THEN HERE ARE MY WEAPONS, KARATE, MY EMPTY HANDS."

Mr. Parker in a promo shot for one of his movies.   Black Belt Magazine

Mr. Parker, considered to be the 'Father of American Karate' is credited with opening the first successful commercial karate school in the United States.

He promoted the **INTERNATIONAL KARATE CHAMPIONSHIPS** in Long Beach, CA, which is an open tournament to **all stylists**, not just those from a select organization or style. Hollywood discovered Bruce Lee, Chuck Norris, Joe Lewis and others there.

Mr. Parker's most famous student was 'The King' Elvis Presley for whom he acted as friend, teacher and bodyguard for 17 years. Parker's system of martial arts is called Kenpo Karate and students worldwide practice Mr. Parker's Way.

Besides teaching his art around the world, Parker made movies, wrote books, promoted his karate tournament and taught seminars. I was fortunate to learn Ed Parker style Kenpo from Mr. Herb Steet, who introduced me to Mr. Parker for the first time at his 1978 Internationals. Regardless of whether other martial artists agree with Mr. Parker's system or not, his contribution to the Martial Arts was tremendous.

These few words are by no means an adequate description of the contributions this man has made to the continuing development of martial arts. I have included what I feel is important for martial artists to know. Like Elvis thought, Ed Parker would be my first choice to protect me in a crowd but I feel a good fighter needs to kick to stay fit and work their cardiovascular system. Mr. Parker died of a heart attack at age 58.

I like this photo of Mr. Parker and me, because he's wearing the same shirt he wore with 'The King' at right. Yay!

Jack Hibbard

Parker stated in his book below, "Remember, no matter how good you become, there will always be someone better. So treat everyone with respect. Make a **smile** and a **handshake** your constant companions."

Ed Parker (right) may have been the martial artist who most influenced Elvis' life. Parker began teaching him in 1960 and continued until just before Elvis' death in 1977.

Mr. Parker leaving a plane with Elvis.

Black Belt Magazine

This is a 'Progressive' system of martial arts. There are basics in kenpo that teach you many ways to use your body as an effective weapon, that you never thought of. It's not for MMA competition but if you need to learn to protect your life, this is a good source of valuable information. A serious martial artist should have this book in their library.

Photo is from a poster promoting the 1978 Elvis Presley Memorial International Karate Championships.

Despite having terrifyingly fast, deadly hands and low kicks, I felt he should have lost a few pounds for his health. I wondered what he could do if he was a bit slimmer and in better condition. Hope he doesn't come back and get me for this. Yikes!

Japanese Martial Terminology

The following information is simply a collection of Japanese terms I thought were interesting. I have either been required to learn some of the terms to advance in belt ranking in judo or I read them somewhere and wrote them in my notebook. They are in no particular order.

Kirisute Gomen – Article XLV of the "Legacy of Leysau" the first Tokugawa ruler.
The bushi or samurai warriors, are the masters of the four classes. Agriculturists, artisans and merchants may not behave in a rude manner towards bushi. The term of a rude man is an 'other than can be expected fellow.' A bushi is not to be interfered with in cutting down a fellow who has behaved in a manner other than to be expected towards the bushi.

This official government sanction permitted the privilege of **"Kirisute Gomen"** or **'killing and going away.'** The strictures of the warrior code however, helped prevent the privilege from deteriorating into a license to kill. Touching a samurai's sword was a grave offense, as was not bowing properly to a samurai. Violations could cost a person their head.

In addition to sword fighting skills, required training for a samurai included playing a musical instrument and either flower arrangement or growing plants such as bonsai. These additional 'soft' requirements were necessary to give the samurai 'balance' to the hard fighting and killing aspect in their lives. Many samurai also practiced calligraphy.

Bu	–	War
Bushi	–	Warrior
Bushido	–	Way of the warrior
Do	–	The way
Budo	–	War way
Nuki Ashi	–	Stealthy step
Karate		Empty hand
Judo	–	Gentle way
Gaman	–	Traditional Japanese virtue of suffering without complaint
Nakzashi		War arrows
Senki	–	War spirit
Rei	–	Bow
Dojo	–	Workout area or home
Sensei	–	Teacher

KHANJO - Fighting spirit

RONIN - A samurai who had no permanent master to serve. Ronin traveled about in search of employment doing jobs suited to their abilities

KAIZEN - Continual improvement

ZANSHIN – Proper mental and physical form giving opponent no chance for the initiative

KAMIKAZE - Divine Wind. A huge typhoon that prevented the destruction of Japan by an invading Mongol army crossing the sea.

SENJO – JUTSU - A deployment of warriors

BUSHI NO NASAKE – Tenderness of a warrior

BUSHI NO ICHI GON – Written contracts were unnecessary for warriors, their word was sufficient.

O MAKAY KHANJO – Additional fighting spirit

SEIRYOKU ZENYO - Maximum efficiency with minimum effort

MULUSAKU – Kill with silence

AKITA INU - Japanese Imperial guard dog. Also used to hunt bear, wild boar, dog fighting and child protection.

RAKI THE GUARD AKITA

FOOD FOR THOUGHT

To be fond of learning is to be near the cosmic knowledge.
– Chinese Proverb

Receive arrows in the forehead but never in the back.
- Japanese Samurai saying

If all your life you live with a clear conscience, you need not fear a knock at the door at midnight.
- Chinese Proverb

A journey of a thousand miles begins and ends with a single step.
-Chinese Proverb

"He who hits and moves away lives to fight another day."
- Muhammad Ali

"Frazier hit me so hard it jarred my kinfolk back in Africa."
- Muhammad Ali

Correct hitting is invisible. An enemy should fall without ever seeing your hands.
- Chinese Kung fu Proverb

The mind is like a parachute; it only works when it is open.
– Ed Parker

If your plan be for 1 year, plant rice. If your plan be for 10 years, plant trees. If your plan be for 100 years, educate man.
- Chinese saying

"The bigger they are, the harder they fall on you."
- Ed Parker

"Uno no es lo que dice, que es sino lo que demuestra ser." "One is not what one says he is, but what one demonstrates himself to be."   - Roberto Duran

"Inside of a ring or out, ain't nothing wrong with going down. Its staying down that's wrong."   - Muhammad Ali

KARMA – Sanskrit word meaning action. Life tendency or destiny, which each individual creates through thoughts, words and deeds. One's actions in the past have shaped one's reality at present, and actions in the present determine in turn one's future. This is the law of cause and effect at work.

"Think positive, it doesn't cost a penny more."   – Angelo Dundee

When a task is once begun,
Never leave it till it's done.
If the labor be great or small,
Do it well, or not at all.
   - Taught to All Time Knockout King - Archie Moore, by his Grandmother.

Apache

Apache is a Yuma Indian word meaning "fighting men" and was probably given to the Apaches by neighboring tribes of Yumas. Named for the region in which they lived, the sub-tribes had their own leaders; thus, there were the White Mountain, Pinal, Chirichua, Jicarilla, Mescalero, and Ojo Caliente (Warm Springs) Apaches. The Apaches moved about searching for food and water, and would be given a new name for the location they were in.

Geronimo was the most famous Apache warrior. Goyahkla was born about 1829 near the headwaters of the Gila River as a member of the Bendonkohe Apaches. In about 1851 he was called Geronimo by Mexicans he was fighting in revenge for the massacre of his aged mother, his young wife Alope, and his three children at the massacre at Kaskiyeh.

At one time the U.S. Army had 5,000 soldiers, which was 25% of the total United States Army, chasing Geronimo and his band of about 50. Geronimo was never captured. Tired of running and fighting, he finally surrendered to Army troops in 1886. It was said that, even as an old man in his 70's and 80's, in his eye was still the 'Tiger Flash.' Geronimo died in an Army hospital of pneumonia after falling out of his wagon on his way "home" and lay in the freezing rain all night. He was buried at Fort Sill, Oklahoma, February 17, 1909.

Geronimo had his medicine-song and great was its power. The song tells how Geronimo goes through the air to a Holy Place where Yusun (The Supreme Being) will give him the power to do wonderful things. He is surrounded by little clouds, and as he goes through the air he changes, becoming Spirit only.

GERONIMO'S MEDICINE SONG

Oh, ha le Oh, ha le	Oh, ha le Oh, ha le
Awbizhaye	Through the air I fly upon a cloud towards the sky far, far, far
O, ha le O, ha le	O, ha le O, ha le
Tsago degi naleya Ah-yu whi ye	There to find the Holy Place Ah, now the change comes over me.
O, ha le O, ha le	O, ha le O, ha le

Much of this information came from Geronimo's Story of His Life, with Stephen Barrett. Duffield and Company, 1906

PREPARATION OF A WARRIOR

To be admitted as a Warrior, a youth must have gone with the Warriors of his tribe on the warpath four separate times. On the first trip, he will be given only very inferior food. With this, he must be contented without murmuring. On none of these trips is he allowed to select his food as the Warriors do, but must eat such food as he is permitted to have.

On each of these expeditions he acts as servant, cares for the horses, cooks the food, and does whatever duties he should do without being told. He knows what things are to be done and, without waiting to be told, he is to do them. He is not to allowed to speak to any Warrior except in answer to questions, or when told to speak.

During these four wars he is expected to learn the sacred names of everything used in war, for after the tribe enters upon the warpath, no common names are used in referring to anything pertaining to war in any way. War is a solemn religious matter.

If, after four expeditions, all Warriors are satisfied that the youth has been industrious, has not spoken out of order, has been discreet in all things, has shown courage in battle, has borne all hardships accordingly and without complaint, and has exhibited no color of cowardice, or weakness of any kind, he may, by the vote of the Council, be admitted as a Warrior. But, if any Warrior objects to him upon any account, he will be subjected to further tests, and if he meets these courageously, his name may be again proposed. When he has proven beyond question that he is a stranger to fear, he is admitted to the Council of Warriors in the lowest rank.

After this there is no formal test for promotions, but by common consent he assumes a station on the battlefield, and if that position is maintained with honor, he is allowed to keep it and may be asked, or may volunteer, to take a higher station, but no Warrior would presume to take a higher station unless he had assurance from the leaders of the tribe that his conduct in the first position was worthy of commendation.

From this point upward the only election by the Council in formal assembly is the election of the Chief. Old men are not allowed to lead in battle. Old age means loss of physical power and is fatal to active leadership. However, their advice is always respected.

GERONIMO 1906

Taken from the book Geronimo's Story of His Life, with Stephen Barrett
Duffield and Company, 1906

Genghis Khan

General Douglas MacArthur said that the soldier couldn't learn his profession solely by practice. Though weapons change, he must go to the past to learn the basic elements of the art of war. Nowhere can he find them better illustrated than in the career of the Emperor of the Mongols almost 8 centuries ago. General MacArthur said, **"Were all the accounts of all battles, save only those of Genghis Khan, effaced from the pages of history…the soldier would still possess a mine of untold wealth from which to extract nuggets of knowledge useful in molding an army."**

Genghis Khan means "Mightiest Ruler" a name he chose for himself, having been named Temujin, Genghis Khan won by conquest, the greatest empire the world has ever known. His empire included most of the then known world, from the Pacific to mid-Europe, and more than half of the worlds population. Genghis Khan had the ability to brush away all traditions, to go straight at a problem with a completely new approach. He could take all the available methods, techniques, weapons, and mold them, in infinite detail, to his purpose. He was the first to organize a nation for the exclusive purpose of waging war, 8 centuries ago. A young warrior was brought up wrestling and learning combat, and taught to shoot a bow as soon as he learned to talk.

The Great Khan's wars were based on speed and mobility. His armies were usually outnumbered, but he usually had the most troops on hand at the actual point of battle. He knew how to divide the enemy's forces and concentrated his own. He was a master of deception, turning up in one place when the foe expected him in another. He won by flanking movements rather than by costly direct attacks. His swift columns would penetrate the opposing armies, cut them into many parts, and then destroy them one by one. He moved past the strongly held fortresses, leaving them to fall later.

He would use propaganda against an enemy to cause turmoil and pit enemies against themselves. Propaganda was used as a weapon of terror. It was regular practice to remind the country he planned to invade of the dreadful things that had happened to others who had resisted the Great Khan. Submit or be killed, he warned. If his foes submitted he marched in and annihilated them anyway. He skillfully used propaganda at home to build morale. He taught his people that the Mongols were a race apart, superior to all others.

Genghis Khan died on a campaign in 1227 at age 66 at the height of his power. The mighty deeds of his life were crowded in to the last 16 years of his life. His war machine rolled on and his Grandson Kublai Khan continued his supreme power. The Mongol empire fell apart in the hands of less able descendants. General MacArthur pointed out that, "Separated from the ghastly practices of his butcheries, his barbarism and his ruthlessness, Khan's unvarying necessities of war are as perilous to ignore in modern times as they were over seven centuries ago."

I believe this story came from Readers Digest decades ago. I regret not saving the authors name to give them credit for writing these words. - JD

Benny "The Jet's" Championship Fighting Rules

These rules are from the book Training & Fighting Skills
by Benny Urquidez, Stuart Sobel and Emil Farkas – Published by Unique Publications.

Never change what works. Grasp whatever you can, be open minded about everything.

Learn what you want to learn, but never close your mind to something different.

Knowing yourself helps you to know others. Never stop learning, never limit yourself to what you think you may attain.

To be in 100% physical shape you must first be in 100% mental shape.

Respect your judgment. Remember you cannot fool yourself. Take defeat as a process of learning. Never degrade yourself by thinking negatively.

If you lose, figure out why you lost and find the defenses which will help you the next time.

In and out of the ring the secret of a martial artist is to control his anger. There is no time for being old fashioned. One must progress.

Learn to train you mind to be ahead of your body. Beat the pain mentally and you can go on forever.

Don't try to be just as good as somebody else, strive to be better. The way you train is the way you react.

Benny 'The Jet' supervising at his Jet Center.
Bob Warren

Wrestlers are used to physically handling their opponents. Benny is shown here in an early full contact karate fight spiking an opponent on their head when throwing them. That's illegal in modern MMA competition. Benny had wrestling experience, which now everyone knows is a good thing. Years ago wrestlers were not respected like they are now due to MMA.

RULES OF DISCIPLINE

Listening creates reflex. Just as a blind man learns to use his ears to react to noise, so must you train yourself to listen, to become aware, to respond automatically.

Balance. Center your weight in yourself. You should always have your weight centered in yourself because only then will you have natural balance.

Good posture creates good vision and focus. To be able to look at your opponent properly from shoulder to shoulder, you must maintain a good posture at all times. Otherwise, your image and focus will be distorted and your judgment will be inaccurate.

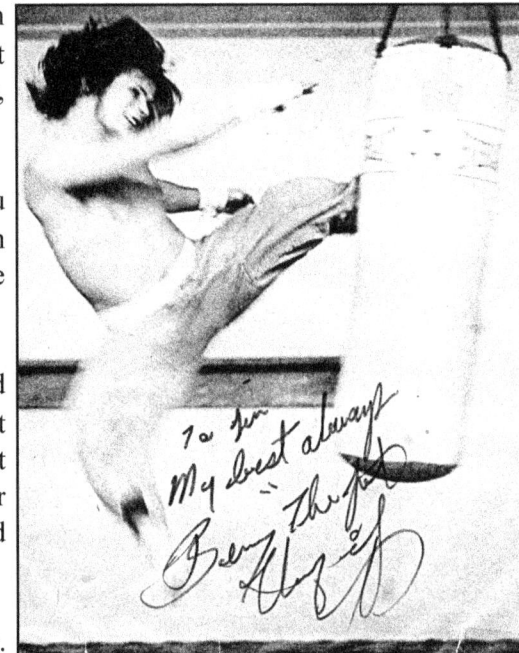

The way you train is the way you react. Train hard in your workouts and you will fight hard in the ring. Don't pull your punches or kicks while you are training and you won't pull them in the ring or in the street.

Coordination. Make your weapons work as one. Train both your hands and feet together. Only then will they work as one coordinated weapon.

Self-confidence. Know you can do it even though you've never tried. You must believe in yourself and your ability. If something new or unexpected is required of you, do it without hesitation. Without self-confidence you have nothing.

RULES OF FIGHTING

Never move back. If you must move back, always do so in a clockwise direction. Never move back in a straight line.

Never set yourself in one spot. Always move around. Make it difficult for your opponent to plan an attack.

Redirect. Never allow your opponent to attack you head on. Always redirect his attacking weapons so that you minimize his offense.

Fight your opponent the way he fights you. Show him that you're better than he is on all levels. That will make him less sure of his own ability.

Place your opponent where you want him. Do this by testing his reactions. Based on this, set him up with faking and feinting techniques. Then go in for the knockout.

Before the Gracie Family was brought to mainstream martial arts attention in 1993 in the first Ultimate Fighting Championship, the World's most famous fighting family I knew of was the Urquidez Family. Judo Gene LaBell introduces them at the Olympic Auditorium.

L to R Arnold, Brother in law Blinky Rodriguez (Bill Superfoot Wallace's toughest fight), Ruben, Benny 'The Jet,' Manuel, and Smiley. World Champion woman fighter Lilly, Blinky's wife, is absent in the photo.

Manuel Urquidez is the first person to beat JD in karate competition at Ed Parkers International Karate Championships in 1978, lightweight black belt fighting division.

Ideals of the United Fighting Arts Federation

Chuck Norris

Code of Ethics

1. I will look for the good in all people and make them feel worthwhile.
2. I will always be in a positive frame of mind and convey this feeling to every person I meet.
3. I will give so much time to the improvement of myself that I have no time to criticize others.
4. If I have nothing good to say about a person, I will say nothing.
5. I shall continually work at developing love, happiness, and loyalty in my family and acknowledge that no other success can compensate for failure in the home.
6. I shall develop myself to the maximum of my potential in all ways.
7. I will always remain loyal to my country and obey the laws of the land.
8. I will be as enthusiastic about the success of others as I am about my own.
9. I will forget the mistakes of the past and press on to greater achievements in the future.
10. I will maintain an attitude of open-mindedness toward another person's viewpoint while still holding fast to that I know to be true and honest.
11. I will maintain respect for those in authority and demonstrate this respect at all times.
12. I will become and remain highly goal-oriented throughout my life.

Creed

1. Discipline - The key ingredient for success in life is the discipline of mind and body. Setting goals, and making sure they are accomplished, builds discipline. Whatever goal I set for myself, I will first get a mental image in my mind of exactly what it is I want to achieve, then I will be determined and persistent enough to overcome all obstacles that get in my way toward that goal. Finally, I will train or study accordingly until that goal is accomplished.

2. Integrity - I will be sincere and honest in my relationships with others and maintain high moral principles in my daily living.

3. Loyalty - I will be faithful, support, defend, maintain allegiance, and be true to myself, my family, my country, my friends and the United Fighting Arts Federation.

4. Respect - I will show my respect for others by following the 12 principles of the Code of Ethics, for respect must be given in order to be received.

Code of Conduct

1. Service - Give unselfish service by helping and encouraging other students, participating in service projects and showing pride in the school by maintaining a clean and orderly place to train.

2. Respect - Students will not only show etiquette for the seniority system and honor senior members, but also show respect for self, other students, and all human beings.

3. Honesty - Our personal, business, family lives will be conducted honestly. No lying, cheating or stealing.

4. Self-Improvement - Develop a habit of lifelong learning by studying books and tapes on success and self-improvement and practicing the principles in daily life.

5. Health - Protect our skills by avoiding harmful health practices such as smoking, drugs, and excessive use of alcohol.

6. Loyalty - Support the Chuck Norris System, your instructor, school and fellow students by word and action.

7. Character - Reflect honor and respect on the martial arts and our association by living a clean and upstanding life.

8. Control - Beginners will mask emotions. Advanced students will control and discipline emotions and actions-act not react.

9. Courage - Develop courage by opposing influences that can cause failure of defeat mentally, emotionally, spiritually or physically.

10. Sincerity - Demonstrate sincerity by carrying the code outside the school and into personal life, not being two-faced or hypocritical.

San Jose, CA Police officer and martial artist Steve Swenson and Mr. Norris. Chuck is a real life Good Guy. His '**Kick Drugs Out of America**' program is just one example of his sincere beliefs in helping others and 'doing good things.' Mr. Norris is an example of a tough guy who is nice, respectful and ***doesn't need to act like or prove how tough he is***.

Steve Swenson

What It Takes To Make A Champion

by Joe Lewis

Joe Lewis training in Okinawan Karate while in the military. He achieved his black belt in 6 months by training intensely most of the day almost every day. Black Belt Magazine

Joe Lewis is making a point to JD. When this man tells you something, you seem to pay attention. George Boyle

"I may not always be by you, but I'll always be with you."

WHAT DOES IT MEAN TO GROW OLD?

What does it mean to age?

Let me tell you about my father. John Gary Lewis. I remember him about the age of 50. Even then, he could work harder than, and outdo, men half his age. The fact that he never smoked or went to the movies or parties made it easier for him, true. But he believed in working regardless of whether he was sick or injured. If he were coming down with a cold, instead of going to a doctor, he would buy a bag of oranges and sit down and eat nearly the whole bag.

The fact is, he almost never got sick and he never seemed to get hurt. He didn't believe in doctors. He was old fashioned in every way: Home care, when you were sick, farming, you name it. He did his plowing behind mules because he thought tractors would damage the roots of the plants. He was a college professor in North Carolina for 30 years, full-time, and when he wasn't doing that, he was out at his farm, working, sunup to sundown, never taking a vacation, day in and day, year after year.

So my four brothers and I grew up in Raleigh in a tough family, guided by the principle that physical strength and endurance are key to survival. I still think of my father at 50 on his feet in the hot burning sun, outworking my brothers and me. A long time afterward, when I turned 50, I got into the ring and sparred four or five rounds with some young kids, three-minute rounds, and I found it quite easy to run them out of gas.

I also happen to have a 62-year old friend, Gene LaBell, a movie stuntman and two-time national judo champion, who can go out on the mat and wrestle nonstop for a full hour. I've seen folks 70 and over who can press their body weight. I know members of the Santa Monica track club-guys 48, 49, and 50 years old-who can still run the 100 meters in 10 seconds flat. The trouble with most of us is that we're conditioned to start surrendering inside once we get between 50 and 60. Our values and interests start to change, and it no longer matters so much who's king of the hill, especially since we know it's unlikely to be us.

But why flush your skills and talents down the drain just because you're a little older? There's something in each of us, call it spirit, an essence, energy, confidence, courage, heart, guts, backbone, intensity, spunk, inner motor, or just plain old refusal to give up, like my old man. If you let this part of you begin to go to sleep, it will begin working on taking the rest of you to your grave.

I have found that each of us has an inner rhythm or gift, and often a great deal of it never even gets touched. We have to learn to live with fear, whether it's fear of failure or plain old fear of being laughed at because we're competing with folks half our age. Common sense and a little reflection make it plain that none of this means a thing.

When you are old, you can still be winner, because winning truly means being the best of what you are, doing the best you can do, regardless of what anybody else says. You don't give up. Like my father, who died at 68 and never gave up, and who has been my life's example. He is no longer by me, but he is always with me.

Never give up. Never.

Joe Lewis
World Karate and Kickboxing Champion

Mr. Lewis passed away in 2012.

Winners vs Losers

When a winner makes a mistake, he says, "I was wrong;"
When a loser makes a mistake, he says, "It wasn't my fault."

A winner works harder than a loser and has more time;
A loser is always "too busy" to do what is necessary.

A winner goes through a problem;
A loser goes around it, and never gets past it.

A winner makes commitments;
A loser makes promises.

A winner says, "I'm good, but not as good as I ought to be,"
A loser says, "I'm not as bad as a lot of other people."

A winner listens;
A loser just waits until it's his turn to talk.

A winner respects those who are superior to him and tries to learn something from them;
A loser resents those who are superior to him and tries to find chinks in their armor.

A winner feels responsible for more than his job;
A loser says, "I only work here."

A winner says, "There ought to be a better way to do it."
A loser says, "That's the way it's always been done here."

PAT WILLIAMS
NBA GENERAL MANAGER AND VICE PRESIDENT

DESIDERATA

GO PLACIDLY AMID THE NOISE & HASTE, & REMEMBER WHAT PEACE THERE MAY BE IN SILENCE. AS FAR AS POSSIBLE WITHOUT surrender be on good terms with all persons. Speak your truth quietly & clearly; and listen to others, even the dull & ignorant; they too have their story. ~ Avoid loud & aggressive persons, they are vexations to the spirit. If you compare yourself with others, you may become vain & bitter; for there will be greater & lesser persons than yourself. Enjoy your achievements as well as your plans. ~ Keep interested in your own career, however humble; it is a real possession in the changing fortunes of time. Exercise caution in our business affairs; for the world is full of trickery. But let this not blind you to what virtue there is; many persons strive for high ideals; and everywhere life is full of heroism. ~ Be yourself. Especially, do not feign affection. Neither be cynical about love; for in the face of all aridity & disenchantment it is perennial as the grass. ~ Take kindly the counsel of the years, gracefully surrendering the things of youth. Nurture strength of spirit to shield you in sudden misfortune. But do not distress yourself with imaginings. Man's fears are born of fatigue & loneliness. Beyond a wholesome discipline, be gentle with yourself. ~ You are a child of the universe, no less than the trees & stars; you have a right to be here. And whether or not it is clear to you, no doubt the universe is unfolding as it should. ~ Therefore be at peace with God, whatever you conceive Him to be; and whatever your labors & aspirations, in the noisy confusion of life keep peace with your soul. ~ With all its sham, drudgery & broken dreams, it is still a beautiful world. Be careful. Strive to be happy. ~~

FOUND IN OLD SAINT PAUL'S CHURCH, BALTIMORE; DATED 1692

Weapon Basics

Since the use of weapons is a large part of martial arts, I will include some elementary ideas and thoughts about them.

Traditional martial arts weapons such as the 6' bo staff, the sai, tonfa, cane, escrima sticks, Korean short sticks, swords, bokken, shurikens, 3 sectional staff, nunchaku, chain whips, knives and other weapons are used by traditional martial artists. All these weapons can be lethal if used properly by someone who is skilled. Some of these weapons can hurt the person using them quite badly if they are unskilled or they make a mistake.

As with anything, each of these weapons have their advantages and their disadvantages. The situation, the environment around you and what your opponent is armed with, if anything, will dictate which of the traditional weapons will be most effective for you. You probably won't have the time to enjoy selecting the appropriate weapon when you need to defend against an opponents weapon.

There are numerous ways training with traditional weapons is beneficial to you. Traditional weapon practice improves your concentration, body awareness, quickness, reflexes, hand-eye coordination, striking accuracy, ability to judge distances and of course overall fighting effectiveness. Any type of hand held weapon, including firearms, are all considered to be extensions of your hand. If you are unable to coordinate your eyes and hands to work together or lack control of your body a weapon will lack effectiveness. A great advantage to traditional weapons training is that you can learn to improvise with many other objects if the actual weapon itself isn't available. You can pick up countless other objects and turn them into useful weapons with the basic concepts behind various traditional weapons.

If firearms are the only weapons you have trained with, it's doubtful you can effectively replace a firearm with just something you pick up, so remember that. Some non-martial artists with firearms, many of whom are overweight and out of shape (OK, they are fat guys) ***are much too dependent on their firearm***. These shooters would be in a world of trouble if they were surprised at close range and didn't have time to draw or access their weapon. They could be caught without their weapon, found it inoperable for some reason, had it dislodged or taken away, had ammo failure or maybe just ran out of ammo.

When I have mentioned this to some non-martial arts shooters, I have sometimes heard the same rationalization some kickers have about being taken down or some grapplers have about getting kicked into unconsciousness. Some people are just certain (in their mind) it could never happen to them.

Many traditional weapons can be picked up at home and at least casually moved around in the back yard, garage or living room, making the weapon feel as though it's part of your hand. Getting any weapon to feel as though it belongs in your hand is a very important part of weapons training of any kind. Traditional weapons usually don't make much noise unless you accidentally let loose of it when practicing and it crashes into something but this is usually not enough noise to concern many people. Losing the traditional weapon while practicing is not good, but can and does happen to many who practice hard in the beginning. Especially in the early stages. Remember: slow is smooth, smooth is fast. So go slowly and carefully at first. Later, if you don't push yourself, you won't become proficient. If you go hard, you should expect to make some mistakes and a weapon can get away from you.

There are usually fewer laws regulating traditional weapons, than firearms. Many people don't like firearms and believe you are a 'gun nut' if you own or practice with a firearm. There are people who believe firearms are just not socially acceptable and believe those who train in the martial arts are aggressive brutes looking to beat up others, so be careful how you train. Obviously, people who think that way don't know the true reason and philosophy behind real martial arts regarding avoidance of trouble. Those folks lack education in these matters and you are expected to always set a good and positive example so others who may have a dim view of what you do may decide to change their minds because of your respectful and courteous behavior.

Despite all the advantages traditional weapons have, we all know they can be very ineffective against modern firearms. That being said, there are situations where a properly trained person using a traditional weapon could easily beat someone armed with a firearm but, all things being equal, the firearm simply gives too much advantage in effective range and power. It doesn't take a rocket scientist to figure that out. Love them or hate them and many people do, firearms are here in America. At least for a while it seems.

I have been asked many questions about personal safety situations at home, such as advice on how to keep the wife and kids safe at home when the husband is away. I ask questions of my own to be able to give them a better answer.

When I ask if they have a firearm available, I sometimes receive an emotional response. Some men and women, get excited and tell me they "Would never have a gun in the house around their kids!" I don't want to disrespect any body's beliefs or philosophies about raising their own kids but it seems to me proper firearm education is

I enjoy young people with proper firearm handling skills. This young lady is much safer to be around than the average teenage girl, and her father feels better knowing she knows how to use a firearm, if she ever needed it.   www.garylewisoutdoors.com
www.americanhandgunners.com

ABSOLUTELY ESSENTIAL to help prevent accidental injury or death when their kids get a little older.

I'm very serious about this subject and want to get this off my chest. My adopted sister's youngest son was accidentally shot in the head and killed because of an **instant of ignorance** by someone else. This was one of those completely avoidable, senseless tragedies and a very tough way for someone to learn. Pay attention!

Protecting kids by isolating them from guns is much like an ostrich sticking its head in a hole in the ground. The ostrich can't see danger so it must not be there. That doesn't work. A good parent teaches a child not to run out in the street because a car could hit them, but they don't hide their kids from cars because they could run them over. Fact is, the leading cause of death for 15 to 20 year olds is from motor vehicles.

The same thing applies to matches, dogs that might bite, sharp knives, poisons around the house, electricity and all sorts of other things. Kids need to be educated about, not just hidden away, from firearms. Keeping kids at home in an environment with no exposure to guns won't prepare them for the future. It's realistic to assume there's potential for kids growing up to be exposed to firearms somewhere, at some point, before they reach adulthood. Even then as an adult they still need to know. An example of that would be the 23 year old idiot who shot and killed his sleeping 24 year old friend in the chest with a real .22 rifle. He thought he would wake him up with the bang, thinking he was using an air rifle. This shooter's parents probably didn't teach him anything about firearms.

PROPER FIREARM EDUCATION is essential and, I believe, should be mandatory. When kids get old enough, they will visit a friend's house. Kids are naturally curious and at some point may see someone else's firearms when there's no adult supervision. This is when accidents happen. Yes, I agree, kids should never be in that situation around accessible firearms without proper supervision but it could be the parents who were not properly educated and allowed it to happen.

So now what? Boys who have been shielded away from guns are often especially curious about them. That's a fact! If he hasn't had this curiosity satisfied because he's always been shielded from guns, he's likely to want to find out for himself what all the fuss is about. Kids see guns all the time on TV and in the movies so what's the big deal? A kid whose parents own a firearm could be showing off to his friends to be cool. The neighbor kid who has never seen a real firearm could pick it up. The exact scenario is widely varied but the result is too often tragic. Someone does something they shouldn't do and the firearm discharges. If everyone is lucky the muzzle is not pointed at a person when it 'goes off.' **"I didn't know it was loaded!"** is the standard thing to hear following such an accident.

O.K. lets back up and say Johnny is over at his friend Ted's house, and Johnny has received PROPER FIREARM INSTRUCTION. He's been trained and has practiced handling and shooting firearms. He's seen what happens to a milk jug full of water when shot, especially with a high-powered rifle. He's seen the water explode into the air, is very impressed and has developed a healthy respect, not a fear, but a respect for firearms.

By the way, **NO!** It's not the same to 'just tell Johnny about the exploding milk jug.' I have heard this lame, whining argument. Johnny knows pretty much what guns can, and can't do. He's been taught since he was a little guy, the **4 Basic Rules** of firearm safety. He understands, can repeat and **explain what the rules really mean,** to someone else.

This is good healthy family fun. These gals are not likely to be out using their handguns for evil. If this mother needs to respond quickly to protect her daughters, it's much more likely she will be successful than a mother who dials 911. Frequent practice is fun, and important for both safety and effectiveness.
www.garylewisoutdoors.com
www.americanhandgunner.com

In the same situation as before with the uneducated kid, if Johnny was at Ted's house, and Ted or any of their friends picked up a parents' firearm, Johnny is going to be much more likely to tell them to **"point that thing in a safe direction!"** He could leave to find a parent or supervisor and wonder if someone is going to get hurt. He could tell them about putting it away or at least check to make sure the gun's not loaded. Yes, I know they have no business having access to the firearm to begin with but this happens.

It seems as though some parents have the idea that because they have firearms around the house, somehow, some way, maybe by osmosis or something, kids or anyone else for that matter, will somehow ABSORB proper firearm safety. It doesn't happen that way. Taking someone out to the gravel pit a few times, talking about guns a bit, doing some shooting, will not replace a REAL FIREARMS SAFETY EDUCATION. Even if a young person doesn't fire a weapon growing up, they still need to know something about them.

A bullet is a very unforgiving thing. An error in most any other subject won't be so serious. Just one instant of forgetfulness, lack of concentration or poor judgment can and does have extremely dire consequences to anyone or thing in the immediate vicinity. In the case of high-powered rifles, the danger zone is within a mile or more away! More on proper firearm safety in the FIREARM SAFETY EDUCATION section. Make sure you learn the correct way. *"Fear not the gun, watch the bullet. – Ed Parker*

FIREARM SAFETY EDUCATION
Teaching the Basics

The first step in learning about handling and shooting firearms should be the evaluation of the person who wants to handle and shoot them.

If it's determined the person is mature enough or with a stable sound mind, fit to understand the seriousness of firearms, then my first step is to make the person write out the **4 Basic Rules** on paper. I can recite the rules so they can write them or if they are old enough, just let them copy the rules on to their own paper.

I do not allow any mistakes in spelling with young students. I make the beginning student start over on a fresh sheet of paper from the beginning if any mistakes are made. I want them to have their own copy to read, memorize and show others. I want the rules to be something young people can be proud to say they wrote with their own hands.

If they are young and it takes half a dozen pages to get it right, guess what? They have spent a good amount of time trying to get it correct. There is no room for errors in this subject, period. There are numerous variations of Firearm Safety Rules. The **4 Rules** I teach are basic common sense, but I read later they are much the same as Jeff Cooper's.

Rule #1
Firearms are always loaded.

Rule #2
Never point a firearm at anything you do not wish to destroy.

Rule #3
Keep your finger out of the trigger guard until you are actually firing the weapon.

Rule #4
Always be sure of your target and what's beyond.

Below is an explanation of the **4 Rules**. I have been told I can repeat myself and this is an example but this is for a good reason. If you practice your bo staff techniques and make a mistake or maybe many mistakes nobody may know. With firearms your first mistake can be your last. There's more to being safe than these **4 Rules**, you can learn that later. My philosophy at the fundamentals level is this: if one strictly adheres to these 4 rules, it's hard to go wrong. Four Rules are short and sweet and cover lots of ground so to speak. They are easy to remember for young and old. A comprehensive Firearm Safety list that's long, complicated and difficult to remember, is about as useful as a series of complicated self-defense movements in a mugging. Simple is effective, remember that!

After these **4 Rules** are copied perfectly and memorized, I ask them what each rule means to them. I start by asking, "What does that mean, all firearms are always loaded?" I ask them if I have unloaded my firearm for cleaning, "How can it always be loaded?"

Beginners usually don't really understand what I mean, but I get them to thinking about what I have said. I explain that if everyone always treated firearms as if they were ***always loaded,*** then there would never be any of those tragic and preventable accidents, where someone goofs around with a firearm, it 'goes off' and someone is shot. No one would be able to say, **" I DIDN'T KNOW IT WAS LOADED!"**

All firearms are considered to be loaded. If everyone always treated firearms in this manner that excuse would no longer be valid. Nobody would accidentally shoot themselves in the leg because they treated the weapon with the respect it deserves. That's why **all firearms are to be considered loaded.** It takes the guesswork out of it. The only exception to this rule is a weapon you personally check regardless of who handed it to you or where you got it. If you pick it up or it is handed to you by your shooting coach and proclaimed to be unloaded, it doesn't matter. Point the weapon in a safe direction (Rule #2) and CHECK FOR YOURSELF.

Remove the magazine, rack the slide 3 or 4 times, open the cylinder, pull the bolt back, what ever the mechanism may be. Visually verify the chamber is empty, then physically stick your little finger in the chamber to feel for a round in good light or poor.

> A final step should **always** be to close the slide, cylinder, or bolt and again pointing it in a safe direction, pull the trigger.

The final procedure is very important. That final pull of the trigger when the weapon is aimed toward a safe area is the way to be absolutely certain it's clear (unloaded). When you have been fatigued, mentally distracted and make a mistake you aren't aware of and verify with certainty with that last 'clear your weapon' step and your 12 gauge shotgun blows a large hole in the floor, you have a tendency to remember it.

Yes, I accidentally did that! It was embarrassing but I was very glad no one got hurt because of that final step. All firearms are always loaded until you unload them yourself. This is a nonnegotiable rule, don't deviate from it, occasionally fudge on it or be lazy just this once. If someone you trust hands you a firearm and tells you it's unloaded, check it. It doesn't matter if it's your dad, check the weapon. A real firearms expert will believe you have received proper training and have more respect for you.

Never point a firearm at anything you don't wish to destroy. Unloaded or not, don't point a firearm at anyone, or any thing. That's important. Except for a ricochet, no one can get accidentally shot if a weapon isn't pointing at them, now can they? You can't accidentally shoot yourself in the foot if it's not pointing at it.

Keep that muzzle from pointing at anything else you want to keep safe, even if it's unloaded, be aware of where it's pointed. Just the extra thought process of being aware of where the muzzle is pointing even when it's unloaded, makes you more aware of that muzzle. Beginners have not developed **muzzle awareness** like those with more experience. Hopefully, you gain respect for that muzzle direction (if you haven't already) in a safe, positive manner, and not the hard way.

Keep your finger out of the trigger guard until you are actually ready to fire the weapon. You must develop a very bad and uncomfortable feeling if you catch yourself with your finger on the trigger unless you have your target in your sights and are about to shoot. You should not walk around, aim or goof off with your finger on that trigger! An exception to this could be dry fire practice but that's a ways ahead for right now. I wish there were a law prohibiting people handling firearms unsafely on TV or in the movies.

Sometimes actors do handle firearms properly. I very much appreciate the actor like Steven Segal or Chuck Norris who have received proper firearm training.

The Navy Seals above or the K9 Police officer (R) are serious professionals, note where their trigger fingers are. If you catch yourself with your finger in the trigger guard when it's not supposed to, you should get a **bad feeling**. If you see someone's finger where it doesn't belong, in person or in the movies, you know they lack training and are a danger to themselves and others. www.surefire.com

Actors should not be depicted sneaking along looking for the bad guy with their finger on the trigger; they should sneak around with their trigger finger straight, out of the trigger guard.

Those life sized posters at the video rental stores and theaters depicting actors with their handguns should be showing their fingers out of those triggers guards, so everyone could see proper firearm handling procedure, instead of extremely dangerous behavior. Movies and television are a powerful influential medium, especially to young impressionable people, so the entertainment industry should set a safe example.

I won't be holding my breath for that to happen. Firearm educators would probably all agree, that by addressing the issue, the entertainment industry would be doing a positive service in the best interest to all who enjoy or need firearms to protect themselves or their loved ones, for sporting competitions, hunting, collections or just shooting cans in the outdoors.

Always be sure of your target and what's beyond. Don't shoot at anything you *think* is what you want to shoot. Only shoot at what you are absolutely, positively *certain* is the target. No thinking, hoping or guessing it's the right target. What's behind and to the sides of your target? If you shoot, are you sure you will hit your target? Will the firearm you are shooting penetrate your target completely with the ammunition you are using and pose a danger if it penetrates completely and exits your target? Will the bullet ricochet off something or bounce back and pose a danger to you or others? Not all of these questions will have an immediate answer in a split second self preservation situation but at least if you know something about your firearm, caliber, ammunition and accuracy, you will be much better off than someone who neither knows or cares.

A father with a .44 magnum in his apartment for family protection should be aware that his choice of weapon has the capability of sending a solid bullet completely thru a burglar, and into his child in the bedroom 2 rooms down the hall. A weapon like that could hit the neighbors in the next block for that matter. The weapon employed needs to fit the environment as well as the shooter.

There are more rules to learn but I'm not writing a firearm safety book so I won't go to great lengths on this subject. If you are ingrained with the **4 Basic Rules,** you are on the correct path and the chances of you getting hurt with a firearm accidentally, will definitely be reduced. Ingrained means the rules are part of the person through usage and frequent practice. Learning something and then not using it frequently is not the same as learning and using that knowledge and skill on at least a fairly frequent basis. If you learn enough martial arts to pass a brown belt test then quit training, before long you won't be able to remember things or move the way you used to. Just think how long it takes to earn a brown belt.

A few casual firearms lessons may not ingrain the type of safety or shooting skills necessary to really prepare you to protect yourself or those you love, should the need suddenly arise. Real self preservation situations usually happens fast and give little time for remembering or skill rehearsal.

*Remember: **Perfect Practice** makes perfect. NOT not practice.*

FIREARM TERMS AND INFO

While teaching basic weaponry to those who have not learned about firearms, I have repeatedly heard the same questions. It's the same with those trying to learn about Hapkido joint manipulations, kenpo techniques, tae kwon do kicking or boxing punches. There are certain inaccuracies and misconceptions many people have about each martial art. If a black belt martial artist has only trained with traditional weaponry, they lack firearm basics and Modern Martial Arts uses firearms. If you're a traditionalist and don't like firearms that's fine with me but regardless of your feelings these weapons are out there.

Some of the following basics are elementary to a shooting enthusiast but some very successful martial artists have surprised me by asking me some of the questions I address below. Just as a shooting enthusiast may not know much about kicking basics, many fighters don't know the simplest things shooters take for granted. Despite its simplistic nature to shooters, I know there are people who have not yet learned these firearm related basics. So to start:

Bullets/Cartridge

A cartridge is a round of ammunition, the thing that's loaded into a firearm. A cartridge consists of 4 components, a bullet, a case or shell casing, propellant or gunpowder and a primer. Among the most common mistakes is using the word 'bullet' instead of cartridge. One can correctly say they are out of ammo, ammunition or cartridges or 'load a round into the chamber.'

An unschooled individual says "I need a box of bullets" when what they need is ammunition or cartridges. The salesperson at the counter selling ammunition understands because they know there are many who don't know or care what the correct terminology is. That's OK, if you don't care, neither do I. If however, you want to be and sound educated, you should learn the proper terms. If you hear someone talk about a kick you know is a roundhouse kick they are speaking of but call it the wrong thing, they sound like they don't know what they are talking about. If you learn proper firearm terminology, those you talk to will have more respect for your knowledge.

So, the bullet is only the part of the cartridge that exits the barrel when the trigger is pulled. Hand loaders buy bullets to seat into the case that is usually made out of brass. They have already inserted a circular little primer in the base of the cartridge case and then loaded the proper amount of powder into the case. When they seat the bullet into the mouth of the case containing the primer and powder, they have created a loaded cartridge or round of ammunition. If they want, they go to the store and buy a box of factory ammunition.

When the cartridge is loaded into a firearm and the trigger is pulled, the firing pin strikes the primer at the base of the cartridge case setting off a spark. This spark ignites the powder in the case, which rapidly burns (not explodes) creating pressure, which forces the bullet out of the shell case and out the barrel. At this point the firearm goes bang!

Handgun terminology

A semiautomatic weapon fires one round each time the trigger is pulled. An automatic weapon continues firing until the finger releases the trigger or runs out of ammo. Many times it's written in newspapers or reported on TV about automatic weapons or machine guns, when usually they are referring to semiautomatic. Either the reporters don't know the difference or don't like guns and want to stir up trouble for gun owners. Sometimes firearm people refer to a .45 ACP pistol as an automatic but it's not a true automatic by definition.

By definition, a machine gun is an automatic and fires rifle caliber ammunition like .223 or .308 caliber. A submachine gun is also automatic but fires pistol caliber ammunition such as 9mm or .45 ACP.

A handgun with a cylinder is a revolver, a semi-auto handgun is a pistol, and a full auto handgun is a machine pistol. All are handguns but I hear the term pistol used when referring to a revolver. This comes from the Old West days when a handgun was called a pistol. Things are different now and the terms pistol and revolver are not technically interchangeable. A revolver has a rotating cylinder that goes around and usually holds about 6 rounds of ammunition. They can hold up to 9 rounds in .22 caliber or 5 rounds in small concealable weapons like .38 snub noses or large powerful hunting handgun calibers like .454 Casull.

Ammunition is loaded into most semi-auto pistols or submachine guns, with a magazine, **not** a clip. A clip holds ammo for a SKS or M1 Garrand rifles for example. By definition a clip doesn't enclose the ammunition like a magazine does and has no spring to push the ammunition to the top.

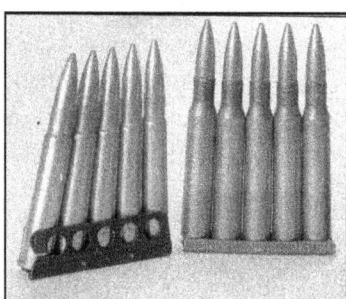

These are stripper clips for rifles. Sometimes the ammo is pushed or 'stripped' out of the clip and into the weapon by hand to load it. An M1 Garrand battle rifle ejects the clip after the last shot.
Mike Venturino, Rifle magazine

Glock 9 mm Sub Compact semi-auto pistol

For many years, the Browning Hi-Power 9mm semi-auto pistol was the most widely used military handgun in the world. At one time it was standard issue to troops of 63 countries worldwide. The

The World Famous Browning High Power 9mm single action semi-auto pistol

FBI Hostage Rescue Team, the British SAS and many other special combative teams have used this pistol.

Also known as the P-35 for the year it was introduced, it was considered an improvement over the 1911 Government model .45 ACP because it was simpler and had the advantage of 13 rounds in the magazine instead of 7 rounds the .45 ACP held.

John Moses Browning

In World War II, every .30 caliber machine gun mounted on boat, airplane, ship, jeep or carried by men, was a Browning designed weapon. John Moses Browning is considered by many to be the most innovative firearms designer ever.

The .45 ACP (Automatic Colt Pistol) is a different caliber from the .45 Colt or the .45 Win. Mag (Winchester Magnum). Most people are familiar with the .45 ACP cartridge produced by Browning in 1904. In 1911 the famous Browning designed 1911 semi-auto .45 pistol shooting this cartridge became U.S. military issue and remained so until replaced by the 9x19mm Beretta in 1985.

Some Special Forces in Iraq and Afghanistan are using this .45 ACP cartridge and pistol today. The letter and numerical additions at the end of a weapon, such as 1911A1 or M16A4, refer to modifications and improvements over previous models.

Single/Double actions

Modern handguns using a double action trigger have replaced many of the single actions due to safety related reasons. The military and police don't have the time to train recruits how to master the single action pistol, especially for personnel with no previous firearms experience. A single action handgun, either pistol or revolver, is easier to discharge accidentally. This is known as an AD or accidental discharge which, as you know, is usually a bad thing.

A single action revolver or semi-auto pistol must be manually cocked before it can be fired. Many expert handgun shooters carry their single action semi-autos 'cocked and locked.' This means full magazine, loaded chamber, hammer back, safety on, or engaged. To fire their pistol, they first have to disengage the safety with their thumb, then pull the trigger. The trigger pull is short and light; the same for each shot. Experts can draw and fire this type of weapon slightly faster and more accurately for the first shot than the double action designed semi-auto.

Double action triggers have a longer, harder pull for the first shot; maybe a 12 pound pull. Each shot after that, the trigger pull is shorter and easier like a single action, maybe a 5 or 6 pound pull. This longer, harder trigger pull for the first shot makes it a fraction of a second slower and potentially not quite as accurate with the initial shot.

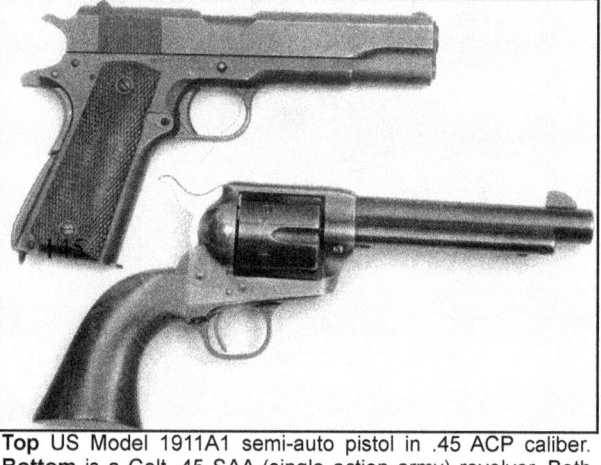

Top US Model 1911A1 semi-auto pistol in .45 ACP caliber. **Bottom** is a Colt .45 SAA (single action army) revolver. Both handguns are single action, and fire two completely different .45 caliber cartridges. Yvonne Venturino, American Handgunner Magazine

There are also Double Action Only (DAO) for those who really want safety. These weapons have the same long, hard (relatively speaking) trigger pull for all shots.

On the positive side, police who must physically control scary bad guys while keeping them covered with their handgun, benefit greatly from the double action. Holding a single action pistol on a dangerous suspect who may be uncooperative and struggling, can unconsciously cause a slight increase in finger tension on the trigger finger resulting in the handgun firing unintentionally.

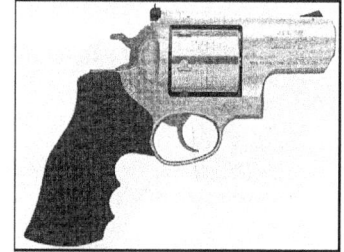

A double action revolver. This is a powerful Ruger Super Redhawk Alaskan in .454 Casul caliber.

This is not good for anyone except lawyers. This is another reason to keep the finger out of the trigger guard until actually firing the weapon. The trigger on a double action is not as easy to accidentally pull, so it's safer for the average person or a police officer trying to control an unruly criminal.

Caliber designations/meanings

Common questions I hear include what those caliber names mean and where did they come from. This is a very large category of information and as I usually tell people, the more you learn about firearms the more you realize how much you don't know. That applies to myself and others interested in firearms, as each year there are many new weapons and related products to keep up with. The following information will help you be more knowledgeable about modern weapons if you are interested in learning more about them.

The usual methods used by Americans to designate a particular name for a caliber are not as useful as the European metric measurement methods. It's confusing to start learning what

Americans mean when naming a new caliber. I will begin with a common former U.S. military caliber, the 30-06. This caliber shoots a bullet .30 inches in diameter and in 1906 was officially adopted by the U.S. Military. This method has some drawbacks. First, the .30 really measures .308 inches but is rounded off to .30 caliber, as are most all .30 caliber designations.

Older calibers, like from the Old West, include the 30-30, 30-40 Krag, and .45-70 Government. The 30-30 has a .30 caliber (.308) bullet and the cartridge case used 30 grains of gun powder. The 30/40 had the same diameter bullet but 10 more grains of powder, so was more powerful. The big .45/70 had a lot bigger bullet and much more gun powder. The gunpowder used in the Old West was not the same as today's modern propellant.

In metric measurements, the same American 30-06 cartridge is listed as a 7.62x63mm. The 7.62 is the diameter of the bullet measured in millimeters and the 63mm is the length of the case. Since it's not rounded off, 7.62mm is a more precise measurement than the American .30 inches measurement. What does the 06 mean to someone who doesn't know about the U.S. Military thing in 1906? Not much.

The European method gives us the length of the case, which in turn gives a ballpark idea of the capacity of the case to hold powder. Usually, the more powder capacity the case has, the more powerful the cartridge potential. The trick to this however, is some cartridge cases are fatter than others and therefore, have a higher capacity to hold gunpowder. So the length of the case can be deceptive for an approximate idea of powder capacity and therefore power, that the caliber has.

In handguns, a 9mm can be one of the following: the 9mm Lugar or Parabellum (9x19mm) which is what most Americans know as the 9mm. There is also the 9mm Makarov (9x18mm) the 9mm Largo or the 9x23mm Winchester. Again the metric measurement gives you more information as to approximate power levels, even here, with less powerful handguns. The 9mm equals .355 inch, relative to the 11.43x23mm (.45 ACP) caliber. The 9x19mm Parabellum cartridge was introduced in 1902 by the Germans for their Lugar pistols. The German word 'parabellum' means 'for war.'

Some modern short action rifle cartridges, such as the .300 WSM (Winchester Short Magnum) have shorter fat cases holding more powder than it may seem. If all you knew was the diameter of the bullet and the length of the case for this big game hunting or long range target cartridge, you could be deceived by its power.

What really gives us an idea of the potential power a particular cartridge has, if you don't have a ballistics table, is a measurement of water, measured in grains, that the empty case holds. Water is used because it is consistent, uniform and easily obtained. Gunpowder comes in different shapes and sizes of granules, so it's too variable to use as a constant for measuring and comparing cartridge case sizes.

Rifle cartridges with short, fat cases tend to be more accurate than cartridges with longer, skinny cases but the average rifle shooter wouldn't really know the difference. Other advantages to a shorter cartridge case is the ability to make a lighter rifle because the action is shorter, making the rifle easier to carry. A shorter case also means the action can cycle rounds in and out of a bolt action, semi or automatic, faster.

Other useful information about a cartridge is knowing the weight and construction of the bullet that particular cartridge uses. There are 99 different factory loads listed in the 2009 Guns and Ammo Magazine Ballistics Table for the 30-06 (7.62x63mm). At the small end of the spectrum, a 30-06 rifle can shoot a 55 grain .22 caliber Accelerator bullet that fits in the .30 caliber barrel with a plastic sabot that falls away after leaving the muzzle. It has a muzzle velocity over 4000 fps (feet per second). At the big end, a 250-grain hand loaded bullet can be fired in the '06. Measured in foot-pounds, the muzzle energy of the thirty-aught-six is about 2900 ft lbs at the higher end of standard factory loadings.

Variations of the old 30-06 military cartridge have been made by using the '06 case and 'necking it down' and putting a smaller diameter bullet in the case. The .25-06 is simply a .25 caliber bullet in the '06 case. The popular .270 Winchester caliber is also a '06 necked down to use a smaller (.277) diameter bullet, but the caliber designation .270 Win doesn't give any clues to its origin or power.

The U.S. Military's M2 .50 BMG caliber machine gun cartridge is a *scaled up* 30-06 cartridge, and the military's M16 rifle fires a 5.56x45mm (.223 Remington) cartridge that is a *scaled down* 30-06 cartridge. The .243 Winchester is a .308 Winchester (7.62x51mm) necked down to a .24 caliber bullet, and a 7mm-08 cartridge is a 7mm bullet in the necked down .308 Win.

Modern developments in gunpowder have made it possible for Federal, Winchester, and Hornady to load factory ammo for selected cartridges, such as the .270 Win. or 30-06 to energy levels equaling the .270 WSM and .300 Winchester Magnum levels without increasing the pressure in the rifle to dangerous levels.

Examples of types of rifle bullets include pointed spitzers, boat-tails, hollow points and stoutly constructed, controlled expansion heavy big game hunting bullets.

Years ago I shot holes completely thru a piece of iron that was a full one-inch thick with some old WWII 30-06 armor piercing ammo. Armor piercing bullets penetrate a substantial amount of material. Military armor piercing bullets, depending on the caliber and country that produces them, have some form of hardened steel, tungsten carbide or other metal alloy bullet core, covered by a copper jacket. This bullet bores right through thin iron without expanding because expansion inhibits penetration. The larger surface area of an expanded bullet requires it to displace more material as it bores thru.

The copper jacket of the bullet peels off the hardened steel bullet core and is shed while it is penetrating material. The copper jacket is necessary to protect the inside of a barrel firing the bullet. If just a hardened steel bullet were fired down the barrel, especially in machine guns, the inside of the gun barrel would quickly be ruined due to friction and heat.

Standard military ammo called FMJ (full metal jacket) or 'ball' ammo, again depending on caliber and country which produces it, has 3 layers. These bullets have a lead core for weight, a hardened alloy or steel jacket around the core for better penetration than the lead core provides and a copper jacket on the outside for barrel protection while it's fired. Ball ammo is very penetrating but not as much as armor piercing ammo is. The penetration of FMJ bullets enables soldiers to shoot thru concealment and hit their enemy. Concealment hides you but doesn't stop bullets. Cover hides you and stops bullets. There are also a number of specialty bullets including tracer and incendiary bullets.

According to information I read, new frangible bullets are being used in close quarter building searches in Iraq by U.S. Marines and are available to the public. This technology makes bullet ricochets less of a danger in close quarters. The new bullets turn to dust when striking a harder surface than the bullet, such as concrete or steel but are lethal when striking humans. These new bullets are created from a mixture of tungsten and nylon or other mixtures. Exposure to high concentrations of lead, especially on military shooting ranges, is also a concern.

In 1954, the caliber that replaced the 30-06 for the U.S. Military was the .308 Winchester. In metric terms it is the 7.62x51mm, also commonly referred to as the 7.62 NATO. NATO forces throughout the world adopted it as the standard rifle caliber for simplicity in providing ammunition to troops from different nations. The length of this case is deceiving in this comparison to powder capacity of the 7.62 x 63mm that it replaced.

Being 12 mm shorter, one could assume the 51mm case would be less powerful. Again, it is confusing. In 1906 the powder available for ammunition was different from the more modern powders in the 1950's. The 51mm case holds more efficient powder than the 63 mm case did in 1906. The difference between the two cartridges shooting the same weight 150-180 grain bullets is only about 100 fps, meaning there's not much difference. The shorter case length of the NATO cartridge allows it to cycle more efficiently in machine guns, and ammo is lighter so soldiers can carry more rounds.

The infamous AK-47 fires a 7.62x39mm cartridge which is not as powerful as the 7.62x 51mm, but at ranges out to 200-300 meters or farther, you will be dead if you are hit in a good spot. It works in war where it's better to wound the enemy than kill him. It requires more personnel and resources to tend to a wounded man, than a dead one. Use up the enemies resources any way you can.

The modern replacement for the 7.62x51mm as the standard issue U.S. battle rifle is the 5.56x45mm or .223 Remington fired in the M16. It first used a 55-grain bullet but now uses a 62-grain bullet for more terminal performance down range. Muzzle energy is about 1300 ft lbs at the muzzle. Again, this is less powerful than its predecessor but it's easier for men to shoot accurately because it doesn't kick as hard. The .223 and military cartridges are almost the same but it's not recommended to fire military ammo in a .223 Remington rifle because the military round is too hot.

These days many recruits entering the military have little or no experience shooting a rifle. A less powerful bullet that hits something is a lot better than a miss from a rifle that is uncomfortable to shoot and makes the shooter flinch. The smaller 5.56x45mm ammo is lighter so riflemen can carry more ammo than 7.62 NATO and machine guns cycle easier because of the shorter cartridge case.

The weapon with the longest continuous U.S. military service is the .50 caliber (12.7x99mm) M2 BMG (Browning Machine Gun). It was first used in 1917 and is still being used by our military.

Used as a rifle cartridge, the Marines call the Barrett .50 BMG caliber semi-auto rifle a SASR (Special Application Scoped Rifle) because technically, to qualify as a sniper rifle, it must shoot 1 MOA groups.

Barrett semi auto .50 BMG
Combat Tactics 2003 www.surefire.com

While the SASR is accurate, in military form, it doesn't quite shoot that well. The Barrett .50 BMG semi-auto rifle is primarily used against light vehicles or lightly armored equipment but hits men too. MOA means 'minute of angle,' which simplified, means about a 1" group per each 100 yards. Examples are 1" group @ 100 yards or 6" group @ 600 yards or 17" group @ 1700 yards.

In war men have sustained tremendous injuries caused by bombs, artillery, grenades, land mines and other weapons. Many seriously wounded men

continued fighting and killing their enemies for some time after receiving large holes in their bodies.

Some men have died later and some have recovered fully. Some of these holes in their bodies were vastly larger than a .45 (11.43mm) caliber hole. **This is absolute fact.**

Knowing it is *factual* that some determined men keep fighting with big holes in them, the 2.43 millimeter sized hole difference between the 9mm and .45 ACP calibers is mostly insignificant to me. The theory of a larger hole of the .45 ACP causing more blood loss and taking an enemy out of a fight faster is not comforting to me. I just plain can't rely on such an insignificant measurement.

A bullet must be placed where it will stop a deadly attacker, because such a small hole placed just any old somewhere in their body doesn't stop a really determined man. Don't think a small little handgun bullet or for that matter a 12 gauge slug will do magic things by itself. One bullet can and will, drop someone instantly but you must deliver it properly for it to do so. If you look at handgun ballistics tables, you can see that the .45 ACP ball ammo and the 9mm ball ammo used by the military has nearly the same foot-pounds of energy. The .45 ACP bullet weighs twice as much the 9mm but the 9mm goes faster. Going back to the physics lessons about mass times velocity squared, this is how the 9mm gets its power.

One thing different about military use and civilian self protection situations is the use of modern high velocity expanding bullets. In war a 9mm ball or non expanding bullet is very penetrating and can zip through your enemy causing a not so serious wound and could only slightly slow down attacker. They may bleed out sometime later after they killed you. The Hague Convention (not the Geneva Convention) prohibits military use of expanding bullets. It's OK to blow the enemy up with a cluster bomb or napalm but don't shoot them with a hollow point bullet!

The .45 ACP with its 2.43mm larger frontal area doesn't penetrate as well as the 9mm. An enemy shot with a .45 ACP is more likely to absorb all the .45's energy because the bullet remained in his body instead of passing thru like 9mm ball has a tendency to do, if something solid in his body is not struck. Civilians can use hollow point expanding bullets. The .45 ACP is more powerful than a 9mm with some of these loads but there is more muzzle blast and recoil. This can and does, affect accuracy and follow up shots for some shooters. Ammo for the 9mm is usually cheaper than many other calibers, allowing one to shoot more often and therefore be a better shot.

Use the most powerful weapon you can control and shoot accurately and effectively. If you are not confident that a weapon will stop someone trying to hurt you, then it's not the best choice for you. With the amazing amount of choices in calibers today, the hard part is choosing one. Among the current most popular handgun calibers for police and civilians, is the .40 S&W. Other modern and effective calibers for semi-autos include the newer .357 SIG, which approximates the .357 Magnum in a smaller cartridge.

This is a .40 S&W case necked down to .357. The new .45 GAP (Glock Automatic Pistol) roughly equals the .45 ACP in a smaller cartridge, so a smaller, more easily concealed weapon holding more ammo is possible.

Don't discount a .22 handgun. You can shoot one all day because ammo is very inexpensive and a .22 is very easy to shoot. You can buy 500 rounds of .22 Long Rifle ammo (also works in handguns) for about the price of 50 rounds of 9mm FMJ. With practice, you should get fast and accurate at close range and the more you shoot the more confident you become, knowing you can hit what you aim at. A .22 is not the ideal defensive caliber and never will be but if threatened, it's possible a 12-year-old girl who has grown up on a ranch shooting a .22 can end that threat with a solid point bullet to the forehead.

I watched an unforgettable TV program on American Sportsman many years ago. Among the shotgun hunters shooting some small fast game birds was General Chuck Yeager. I can't remember the type of game bird but I remember there was an American Indian armed with a recurve bow and arrows, in the group of shotgun hunters. The Indian was shooting those fast, small flying birds, out of the air right along with the shot-gunners and sometimes beating the shot-gunners.

That showed me that it's NOT THE WEAPON that's so important. Many people have heard the saying 'It's not the gun, it's the gunner.' **This guy didn't even have a gun!** It was an amazing example of what a person who practices a lot can do with, by modern standards, a laughable weapon. It was unbelievable but true. I have read that Eskimos would lay on the ice with a .22 rifle using themselves as bait for a polar bear. When the bear gets close enough the Eskimo would shoot the bear in the eye and kill it. Don't try that at home. That would require plenty of confidence and to get that confidence they had to practice. Eskimo's didn't have much money for rifles and ammo so they made what they had work; their very existence depended on it.

How much power?

A ballistics table lets you see what kind of velocity, energy and bullet drop a caliber has. If the idea of knowing what different loads in different handgun and rifle calibers offer in the way of power and trajectory, then ballistics tables give you what you need to compare calibers. The three types of ballistics are internal, external, and terminal. Internal ballistics relates to the pressures and forces of a cartridge in the chamber when fired. External ballistics refers to the flight of the bullet when it leaves the barrel, including the velocity, energy and drop. Terminal ballistics covers what happens to the bullet when it hits the target.

For those who are so inclined, the formula for figuring foot-pounds of energy is as follows: Bullet weight measured in grains, times velocity squared, divided by 450,240.

For those interested in learning more about firearms for defense, shooting, hand loading and such, I recommend a few of my favorite gun writers. Massad Ayoob, Chuck Taylor, Leroy Thompson, Rick Jaimison, Clint Smith, Evan Marshall and Col. Jeff Cooper who passed away in September 2006. These men will take you far beyond the elementary information presented here.

**World Class Firearms Training 2017
Thunder Ranch in Oregon**

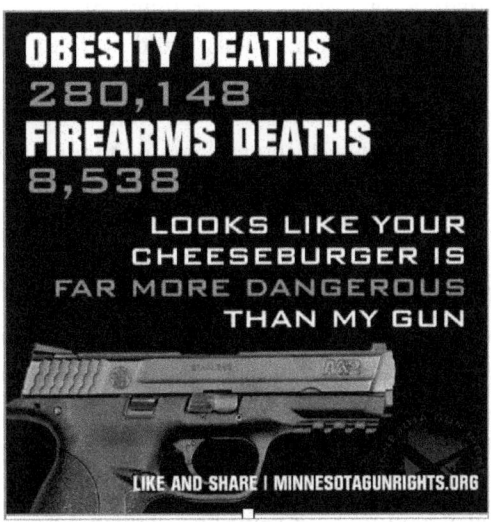

MIND SET

After years of reading, learning and practicing, there's always the standard argument that will never be resolved regarding which is 'the best.' This could refer to different types of fighting styles, as well as the selection and use of a weapon system for personal defense.

There are many martial arts practitioners who are not very familiar with firearms. Many believe they have more knowledge than they really do. I don't know everything, don't claim to know everything, never will. I am always learning, but I am sure of a few things. One thing I am sure about is the use of the mind to keep a person safe. I'm going to touch on handgun and ammunition selection to help a person remain safe in today's society.

It's obvious that martial arts styles are very different and one style may be much better suited for some individuals than others. The same goes for firearms; different situations obviously call for different weapons. A person's size and ability to control a firearm and their experience shooting, are among the many variables. Home defense will be a different situation from the person legally carrying a firearm for personal defense outside the home.

A professional security person's needs are more demanding than a private citizen who lives, or works, in a relatively safe area. A shotgun is much more effective than a handgun in most home defense settings but may be too large and powerful for an older or smaller person. A shotgun can't be easily or conveniently carried around by someone wanting to be safe on the streets.

MINDSET

Regardless of the situation, or firearm and ammunition selection, the single most important aspect in remaining safe is MIND SET. This is old news to experienced firearms people, but many others either haven't been taught, or don't seem to get it. After reading a lot about controversial subjects such as 'which is best,' a 9mm, a .357 magnum, or a .45, etc., I asked retired Brigadier General Charles Bushong what his thoughts were about the Army switching from .45 caliber handguns to the 9mm years ago. General Bushong is a very nice man, having invited me to his home and spending his time answering many of my questions.

Since General Bushong had served in World War II, Korea, and Vietnam, I believed his actual wartime experience regarding these matters carried maximum weight. When I asked him this question he suddenly reverted to his Army General Voice, answering in a profound way. His response was loud and to the point, leaving no doubt or reason for me to ask about it further. *"It doesn't make a damn bit of difference whether you use a .38, a .45, .357, or a 9mm, it's where you hit them that counts!"* I know it would matter which caliber you are using if you make a semi-bad shot in some situations, and there are many variables, but the moral of the story is not to get so concerned about the details of the particular type of handgun, caliber and ammunition. Hit your target accurately, which sometimes is not very easy to accomplish if someone is moving around trying to kill you.

Back to MIND SET. The best scenario would be that you are armed with the very finest weapon suited for your personal use, loaded with the most proven effective, high tech ammunition; however, if you aren't paying attention to your surroundings and someone try's to hurt you, it won't matter what you are armed with. Chances are you will be hurt or worse. If someone attempts to harm you, a proper MIND SET is mandatory for remaining safe.

You must be prepared to do something about the danger. Just because you are aware of what's happening around you, doesn't mean you have made the mental decision ahead of time to be psychologically ready and able to respond to deadly force *with* deadly force. There are people who for one reason or another don't have it in them to use deadly force.

I'm not going to make a judgment on their personal beliefs. I just want those who haven't thought about this to consider it before a potential situation develops. As a "Martial arts guy," (Grand Master Ji term) I like to think positively. I like to think and teach that odds are; it ***probably won't*** happen to you, but it's naïve to go about life thinking it ***can't*** happen to you.

Having thought about what you need to do in a real life situation before it happens to you, could spell the difference between reacting properly and freezing up in shock and disbelief, wondering what to do. Remember 'bad people,' who harm others, don't think like the good folks you are hopefully associating with. Real bad people don't pause and wonder if it's the right thing to do before they cut, club, rape or shoot you.

Real bad people are like the predators you see on the Nature Channels. Those predators are looking to eat, and since, in nature, they can't go to the supermarket, they kill something to eat. Many times they miss the kill and sometimes they get hurt biting off more than they can chew. Predators in nature don't see anything wrong with what they are doing; if they did they would starve to death. Well, there are predators in society who harm others to get money or drugs and sometimes they kill because they think it's fun. They may rape you before they kill you and sometimes they rape you after they kill you. Sometimes, being the same sex as you, is just fine with them. Again, this probably won't happen if you lead a good clean life and do good things with good people.

If you spend time studying violent crime and who it happens to, the more you realize it can happen to the very best of people. A few examples are: Bill Cosby or John Walsh with their sons, or Michael Jordan with his father. Victims of violent crime you see on TV or read about, didn't wake up one morning and think to themselves "Hey, I believe today's the day I get myself mugged!" It seldom happens that way.

Victims are usually shocked, surprised and think it only happens to 'the other guy.' Well, the folks you hear or read about in the news think YOU are 'the other guy.' Your mind is your most important weapon; it must be alert to what's around you like the animals in nature. Animals are alert because failure to do so is fatal. You must also decide if you have it in you to resist deadly force *with* deadly force.

Remember, deadly force used against you or someone you care about, is usually the ONLY reason for you to use deadly force such as a firearm against someone. Spending time in prison for an unjustified beating or shooting probably won't be your idea of good times in fun places.

The definition of when to respond to deadly force, can include your fear of grave bodily injury or death from someone with a weapon, or who is much larger and stronger. If someone is capable of inflicting such injury to you without the use of a weapon, you could still be justified. This is a legal matter and individual situations are as complex and varied as there are people. You are best advised to consult your local and state laws regarding use of deadly force and what your rights are. Find out when you can and can't use such force beforehand. Waiting until you are in a jam, then wondering what your rights are, isn't the best plan for survival.

TACTICS

After MIND SET in a deadly situation whether armed or not, is TACTICS. You can be aware of your surroundings, recognize what's going on and be mentally prepared to prevent yourself from getting hurt. You can have the very best firearm and ammunition available, but if you use poor tactics, you can get yourself hurt or worse. An example of poor tactics would be not finding cover to protect yourself if someone shoots at you. Another is thinking you are going to do something wonderful instead of finding cover quickly. An example of good tactics I will always remember is a story I read by veteran firearms trainer Massad Ayoob.

A 12 year old boy was home upstairs in a two story house, and for whatever the reason, a man armed with a submachine gun entered the ground floor of the house and shot and killed his parents. The boy had received training on how to use his .22 handgun before this incident. He retrieved the .22 and hid behind a bedroom door. When the armed intruder who killed his parents entered the room, the boy shot him in the back of the head and killed him. The 12-year-old boy survived only because of good TACTICS and SHOT PLACEMENT, not because he had the latest wonderful handgun loaded with the latest high tech ammunition. This is an excellent example of clearly being out gunned. Who among you would bet on a 12-year-old boy armed with a .22 handgun to survive against an adult armed with a submachine gun? Any takers? Not me!

Another good example from Ayoob of TACTICS over coming superior odds, involved three men armed with two 12 gauge shotguns. One shotgun was a pump, the other a semi-auto and a .357 magnum revolver. These three armed men attempted to rob one storeowner armed with a 9mm Browning Hi-Power handgun, and he defended himself. The results were quite surprising. The owner shot and killed two of the robbers and seriously wounded the third.

Who would have bet on one store owner armed with a 9mm handgun, against three robbers, each armed with a weapon more powerful than the store owner? I would not have bet on the store owner in these circumstances, but the owner was apparently mentally prepared to defend himself, was alert to what was happening, used great TACTICS and shot straight and fast. That type of thing doesn't happen very often. The store owner was lucky and the robbers were possibly not too sharp, or the storeowner was a prepared serious fighting man determined to go home to his family.

SHOT PLACEMENT

After MIND SET and TACTICS, is SHOT PLACEMENT. If you are forced to shoot an attacker, being armed with a .454 Casull handgun won't help you much unless you hit your target, even it's muzzle energy is about twice as powerful as Dirty Harry's .44 Magnum. It is possible the Casull's muzzle blast may scare the daylights out of an assailant. He may hightail it and find someone else easier to pick on.

That noise may not stop a determined attacker; however, it may be necessary to give them 'lead poisoning' by hitting your target. Having a firearm you can shoot accurately and with confidence, is light years ahead of a weapon that's more powerful, but you can't shoot well because it has a blast, kick and ball of fire belching from the muzzle, making you fear the darned thing.

FIREARM/CALIBER/AMMO

Next in order of importance, is the type and manufacturer of handgun, its caliber and type of ammunition. Much of what you may hear people discussing revolves around these subjects. Seldom do you hear non-firearm professionals discussing MIND SET or TACTICS. You may hear some talk of SHOT PLACEMENT, but unless they have been properly trained, you rarely hear much except what type and caliber of gun they have. They debate caliber but may not even care what type of ammunition the gun is loaded with. Many are quite content if the ammo is the correct caliber to go BANG. Those who argue about the caliber and firearm maker are missing the boat and have their priorities wrong.

These folks should be most concerned with improving their knowledge, skills and abilities. Most modern firearms available today are reliable, and if one spends some time learning about a handgun that's been on the market for a reasonable time, you can probably count on it. Of course, testing and practicing with a favorite handgun to be sure it fits and feels good in your hand, shoots straight and functions reliably makes you feel much better.

The important things for those who have not received proper firearms training include practicing armed *and* unarmed skills, and being mentally alert and aware of their surroundings. It helps to give some thought before hand to situations and environments you place yourself in and what you could do in different situations. Considering the whole idea of what to do before something bad happens, cuts your reaction time.

Not giving an assailant an easy target is much of the battle. If you appear confident and prepared because of proper training, it could cause an attacker to go elsewhere and pick on a less able victim. Remember, in the natural world, predators seek the old, sick, injured or young before they try to tackle the strong and fit. Predators use caution knowing if they are injured while attempting a kill, it could cost them their life. If a cheetah injures its leg and can't run full speed, even if the injury itself is not life threatening, it may result in starvation if it can't catch something because its leg hurts.

Human predators usually do the same thing and try to avoid getting themselves hurt. Exceptions to this are those not thinking clearly, or at all, because of drugs, alcohol, stupidity, mental illness or rage. Human predators usually pick a victim who appears less likely to be capable of defending themselves.

I don't want to suggest that the make and caliber of handgun, brand and kind of ammunition is of no importance. I am always eager to read about and shoot new high tech ammunition being developed. I read with interest what Evan Marshall and Ed Sanow have learned researching the effectiveness of new technology regarding bullet design, and how it really works on people in real life shootings.

Personally, I'm not concerned with extrapolated theories men have about what the effectiveness of a particular load should be. It's good to know about new things, but I don't get all excited about handgun ammunition doing something it can't do without me doing my part first.

To sum up this chapter on Mind Set, I will repeat myself because repetition is of vital importance in teaching and learning. Most important in serious self-defense is:
MIND SET
- The mental alertness, intelligence and awareness of the environment around you. The education ahead of time to know what rights you have and don't have; and the discretion to know when and when not to shoot in a particular situation. The mental decision ahead of time to do whatever is necessary for survival.

The gumption, intestinal fortitude (or guts if you will) to continue fighting even if you are injured or shot, so the assailant doesn't kill you. Education regarding what to do and say, as well as what not to do, or say, afterwards if, God forbid, you need to respond to deadly force in defense of yourself or someone you love.

TACTICS -
These are mostly learned behaviors that could come reflexively due to good thinking and proper training. Evasive action, efficient use of cover or concealment, proper use of lighting, deception or surprise.

Using the environment to your advantage somehow, being sneaky and stealthy. Using your natural senses to see, hear, smell or maybe even feel an enemy's energy. Tactics can also include using your unarmed skills if you are close and good enough. In some situations unarmed skills can be much faster than trying to draw or present a firearm.

Remember the key words here, CLOSE ENOUGH. Depending on the situation, you must move first, forcing them to react to your action. You must know you are going to be hurt badly if you do nothing, then you have nothing to lose if you react unarmed. It's possible to beat someone holding a gun on you but you must have very good technique, perfect timing, be close enough and very quick. A distraction of some type in this situation is most desirable and you must have practiced exploding into action.

SHOT PLACEMENT -
In Theory this is not as complicated as the others; put a bullet, or bullets, in an assailant's body where it stops them, which can be very difficult. The best spot to achieve this goal is the central nervous system, but it may not be easy to hit, if the attacker is stabbing you or shooting at you from behind cover or concealment.

People can be shot in the head but if the angle is too slight, the bullet can glance off and not penetrate the skull. The spinal cord is relatively small, and deep in the body from a frontal shot. The center of mass is usually the accepted target to aim for. Many shooting schools teach students to target the center of mass with two quick shots, called a double-tap, then quickly look and evaluate the effects. If hostile action hasn't ceased, switch targets to the head or pelvis and continue firing until the hostile action has ceased or you run out of ammo.

The pelvis is a support structure responsible for keeping a person standing upright. Breaking down their support structure can make them collapse, causing the attack to stop, unless the assailant has a firearm and is tough and determined to shoot you while he's down.

Serious students of firearms for self defense know some people can be and have been, shot many times before they cease being a danger to others. There's substantial documentation detailing failure to stop (soon enough) determined men who have received fatal heart wounds from weapons including 12 gauge shotguns loaded with 00 buckshot. The men died but not nearly as quickly as those shooting at them wanted them to.

Unconsciousness can take as long as 20 seconds before they bleed out and their brain ceases to function due to lack of oxygen. Twenty-seconds when someone is enraged and shooting, stabbing or clubbing, could be just plain too long! Adrenaline, drugs or alcohol can contribute greatly to a persons ability to continue to fight long after 'common sense' says they should lie down and die.

On the other hand, there are documented cases of men going into shock and dying because they received minor, totally survivable gunshot wounds. Apparently because they were shot, their minds told them they were supposed to die, so they did!

While in foot pursuit of bad guys, police officers have been shot at, had their legs buckle, and have collapsed to the ground saying they had been shot. Despite the bad guys missing their target and the police officers not being hit, the officers' minds have told them they had been shot, so down they went, their brains convincing their legs they should collapse because a bullet hit them!

The mind is extremely powerful. Use it to your advantage!

AMMUNITION

"Fear not the gun, watch the bullet." - Ed Parker

If a firearm is to be used for self-defense, it might as well be loaded with the most effective ammunition for the intended purpose. As discussed elsewhere in this book, the ammunition is NOT the most important element but if you are serious about defending yourself or those you love, why not be informed about the most effective ammo to accomplish the task?

Since ammunition is a broad topic and you need to start somewhere, I will begin with handgun ammunition. As with most topics, there are different philosophies regarding which type of ammo is better and this is true for handgun ammo as well. There are those who believe in the large diameter heavier bullet with more momentum and those who believe in the lighter faster bullet with more shocking power.

First, there is no such thing as the 'best' ammo. There are situations you could find yourself in where one type of ammo would perform more effectively than another type of ammo in the same caliber, depending on the situation. For example, law enforcement is more likely than private citizens to shoot at bad guys that are shooting at them or fleeing from them in vehicles.

Officers may need their handgun bullet to penetrate a vehicle windshield, side glass or car door and then stop the bad guy from escaping or shooting them. Their bullet may need to penetrate some drywall or other obstacle a bad guy is hiding behind. Their bullet must be tough enough not to fall apart on the obstacle, then penetrate the bad guy sufficiently to stop him.

Some ammo is better at penetration than others. Military 9mm ball ammo, also known as full metal jacket (FMJ) ammo is very good at penetration. The disadvantage to FMJ ammo is that if you need to shoot a tough, aggressive, smaller framed person, especially if he's full of drugs, alcohol or adrenaline, a 9mm FMJ bullet may zip in one side of him, and right out the other side.

If no major bones are struck, then a wall, an innocent person or whatever else is behind the little guy will absorb a good percentage of the non-expanding bullet's energy. Only a couple of small holes will be in the bad guy and he may go for some time before he runs out of blood.

In this particular situation with a smaller guy with no cover to penetrate first, a light weight expanding bullet should strike the little person, expand or fragment and cause a much larger wound channel or even additional wounds from bullet fragments. This type of expanding bullet is much more likely to remain inside the person causing them to absorb all the bullet's energy. This is a good thing if you want a bad guy to stop sooner as opposed to later.

According to statistics, private citizens needing to shoot in self-defense find close range frontal shots are usually the norm and are much less likely to need to shoot through obstructions to reach the bad guy.

In the opposite situation of the smaller guy after you, is the 300 lb bad dude with a lot of muscle or fat. A light, fast expanding bullet may not penetrate far enough and stop short of any vital organs. Depending on where it strikes, that type of bullet may just leave a shallow, nasty surface type wound that a mad tough person may not be bothered much by, at least not for a while. That may be long enough for them to beat you to death before he thinks about his pain.

In this big bad guy situation, a heavier, more stoutly constructed bullet will be needed to penetrate farther to reach the huge guy's vital organs. The smaller, faster bullet that would be better for the smaller guy may have more shocking power but the muscle or fat on a large guy may absorb the shock and dissipate the energy through out all that body mass. The internal organs may not receive the shock. It's much like punching a big fat guy in the belly; it doesn't work as well as it does on a skinny guy. I think some guys who shoot but don't trade blows empty-handed, fail to grasp this.

Shooters have different philosophies on which type of bullet is best. It's much the same as which style of martial art is the best. I can't understand why, in today's age of available information, some people can't figure out that sometimes this is best and sometimes that is best, depending on the situation. The heavy bullet fans reason that a large diameter bullet creates a larger permanent wound channel; therefore, causes more bleeding, tissue destruction and has more momentum and knock down power.

The lighter, faster bullet fans know those kinds of bullets create more shocking power and larger temporary tissue stretch cavities. Shock absolutely can affect the central nervous system and if the size of the person shot is relatively proportional to the size and speed of the bullet that strikes them, it can have an instant effect. Waiting until a person runs low on blood and loses consciousness from a large diameter hole can take way too long. If the attacker is too big, the shock from a light handgun bullet to the body may not be enough.

Hunting Lessons

I learned a great deal about bullet performance from hunting. Bare with me here, you will soon see where I am going with this hunting stuff and what it has to do with War Arts. Deer are very similar in size and basic construction as humans and trying to stop a deer will teach you valuable lessons. I will share a few with you.

I remember as a kid reading hunting stories written by Jack O'Conner. He liked to use a rifle in .270 Winchester caliber. He wrote about shooting deer sized game in the chest with a 130-grain bullet and the animals dropping in their tracks from a thing called hydrostatic shock. At the time I had no idea what hydrostatic shock was but I enjoyed his hunting stories. Later when I became old enough to go big game hunting myself, I was interested in anatomy and how bodies are put together. I enjoyed doing a necropsy, of sorts, to the deer that others or I had shot.

It was always interesting for me to see what the bullets did inside the animal's body. I enjoyed seeing how the internal organs and muscles looked, how the tendons and ligaments attached. Knowing what muscles or leg joints look like helps you understand how you are built and understand your body. Grabbing a deer's trachea and feeling it, lets you know roughly what mine or yours is like. It's better than anatomy class in high school because deer are built a lot more like people than the frogs or cats I dissected in school.

When I started buying my own ammunition for my deer rifle, which was a 30-06, I was asked what grain of bullets I wanted. I picked the 180-grain Remington Core-Lokt, which is a heavier, more solidly constructed bullet than what I needed for blacktail deer but I didn't know it at the time. My thought was that 180-grain bullet must hit harder than a 150-grain bullet because it's bigger, so the heavier bullet must hit harder. I wanted to hit those deer hard, so I could enjoy some wonderful healthy venison. My first 7 deer were shot either in the heart, the backbone or both. I couldn't believe how tough those deer were!

I shot my first buck at about 15 yards right in the heart. Imagine my surprise when he just took off running as if I missed completely. As he ran off I shot him in the spine and of course he dropped instantly. As I was doing my usual exploring inside the deer, I could not imagine how that buck could continue running as far as he did up a hill, over logs and bushes, with a blown up heart and a big hole all the way through him. That's how I shot deer in the heart and backbone; they wouldn't stop like I wanted them to even after they were shot through the heart.

Experience will later teach me that a follow up shot on a properly hit deer is unnecessary, but at first you expect the deer to flop over dead from a heart shot, especially at close range, with a rifle that will punch a hole thru an inch of iron with an armor piercing bullet. The deer would usually run down hill into the thickest brush. They could run about 100 yards sometimes and I would have to drag them back up the hill by myself which is very difficult. I respected those deer and believed those animals were amazingly tough!

One day I was out hunting with my brother Matt and I watched him as he shot a buck with a .243 Winchester using an 80-grain hollow point bullet. He fired his rifle and the buck dropped like he was running on electricity and someone pulled the plug. "Wow!" "Must have hit him in the spine!" I thought! Upon my usual postmortem examination, I discovered the buck was hit in the chest area but not anywhere special as far as vital organs. I wondered what happened?

I learned what *hydrostatic shock* was from watching what a little .24 caliber BTHP (boat tail hollow point) bullet weighing a mere 80 grains did. The difference between my larger tough bullet (.30 caliber 180 grain tough bullet, going about 2700 fps feet per second with about 2900 ft lbs of energy) and Matt's little bullet (.24 caliber 80 grain lightly constructed bullet going about 3200 fps with about 2050 ft lb of energy) was his bullet stayed in the deer whose body absorbed all the bullets energy.

Simply put, hydrostatic shock is what happens when a high speed bullet hits flesh or maybe a milk jug full of water. A human is made up of about 70% water and when hit by something going fast, it causes the water to sort of explode inside the body. Similar to a rock thrown into a pond, a wave of energy is transmitted outward. The water in the body transmits this tremendous shock wave, whacks the nervous system and causes instant collapse. Sometimes this means a deer will not take a single step or even fall on its side. It can drop straight flat down without its hooves leaving the prints they made in the dirt.

My bullets were too heavy and solidly constructed for the animal. They slightly expanded and punched a small hole in the ribs in and out as it exited the other side. Since the bullet didn't stay in the deer, it didn't absorb all the bullets energy; the dirt behind the deer absorbed much of it. Even if my bullet blew up the deer's heart and Matt's bullet did not hit the heart or really hit anything special, his bullet worked much faster. My bullets were placed more accurately, had more energy, were larger diameter and were more than twice as heavy.

Matt's bullet killed instantly because the shock to the nervous system shut things down with the same effect as my spine shots. At the time I didn't know the ballistics part but I knew my 30-06 had much more power. That experience made me want to learn why that happened. I began learning about ballistics, bullet construction and placement. I knew the deer I was examining were roughly the same size as humans with relatively light skin or hide, not like an elk, or rhino. I had spent much more time and energy than I wanted dragging my deer back up mountains because they ran off when shot through the heart and it really bothered me why that happened.

I understand why shock works from knocking out people by catching them on the 'button' with a punch or kick and affecting their nervous system. It shuts them right down. It's from a different reason of course and the people wake up. A good punch doesn't have anywhere near the energy a high-powered rifle bullet has either. I try my best to stay out of trouble so I have never shot a person and don't want to try; however, I can easily envision a mean determined person will keep right on stabbing or shooting after being shot in the heart.

Before they run out of blood, bad guys can do terminal damage. I really understand that after watching heart shot deer run away, then having to spend so much time and energy dragging them back up a hill. I don't have much faith in tissue damage and blood loss after relating what a deer can do after receiving tremendous rifle bullet wounds that ***no common self-defense handgun bullet can ever dream of inflicting.***

I realize deer are not people; and rifles are not handguns but I can imagine that in the time it took for those deer to finally quit, if they could have shot back, I could have been in big trouble.

There are educated people who attempt to determine which handgun ammunition will be the most effective at stopping men. There are mathematical formulas and exotic extrapolations designed to predict which will be the most effective. The FBI has a theory, as do a number of others. The man that has done the most actual research on the subject to my knowledge is Mr. Evan Marshall.

Shooting enthusiasts know of him because he is widely read and highly regarded. Some extrapolators don't like him because his factual research differs from their pet ideas. The handgun stopping power debate is much the same as some in the martial arts who don't like some other style of martial arts, because it differs from the style they train in.

Mr. Marshall is a retired Homicide Investigator and SWAT instructor from Detroit. He has spent 20 years researching what happens when bullets meet humans. His research information has not been derived from war stories, bull sessions, shop talk at the local gun store or what his buddies or relatives think. He has taken it upon himself to investigate real life shootings. He would interview witnesses, doctors and attend autopsies. He would talk to the guys who did the shooting and those who were shot but not killed if he could. He compiles the information and assigns a one-shot stop percentage number to a particular load, for a particular caliber.

Mr. Marshall's research work, by its very nature (people shooting each other) is not an exact science. It's not about being able to duplicate things exactly the same controlled way that laboratory science can duplicate things to prove or disprove something. There's some debate about the 'one shot stop' methodology and all the various ways someone can be shot and how many times they can be shot and so on. This 'one shot stop' way of measuring ammunition effectiveness is not a perfect science nor will it ever be. To my way of thinking it's just plain the best information we have, because it's real.

There are those in the scientific community such as the International Wound Ballistics Association (IWBA), who oppose Mr. Marshall's work. Some laboratory scientific minded folks can't seem to either appreciate or comprehend Marshall's research information because it lacks exact laboratory repeatability; therefore, his work (in their minds) lacks scientific basis.

Mr. Marshall's critics want to find flaws in his research probably because Marshall's work detracts from their own conclusions. Bottom line is this in my book.... Look fella's, Marshall's work is not perfect. It is however, REAL and the BEST information there is. If you are curious about things like effectiveness of various calibers and factory cartridge loads, find Mr. Marshall's books and read them.

Paladin Press has **Handgun Stopping Power The Definitive Study** and **Street Stoppers**. These books are co-authored by Evan Marshall and Ed Sanow who is a trained engineer and police officer. Information they provide will help you determine how firearms ammunition can provide safety for you and those you love.

SHOTGUNS!

Tony 'The Warrior' at work with his 12 gauge. He trains his department's SWAT team and I teach him to use his natural weapons. I enjoy 'The Warrior' watching my back at events. Note: his finger is **not** in the finger guard.

Shotguns are awesome defense weapons commonly ranging in size from a relatively small .410 gauge to a 10-gauge magnum firing 3 1/2-inch shells. I held an old 4 gauge commercial goose-hunting shotgun used long ago. It was much too large to be shoulder fired; it was as tall as I was. Many years ago it was laid across an oar lock in a rowboat, and fired at a flock of geese floating on the lake. That's against the law today, of course, but in those days there were no Fish and Game laws as we know them. That weapon commanded respect; unfortunately it was used in a disrespectful (to the geese) way.

Shotguns have the versatility of being relatively small, in the legal form of an 18" barrel with a pistol grip, out to about 36" barrels on modern 10 gauge magnum goose guns. Any shotgun larger than a 10 gauge has been illegal in the United States since 1913. These goose guns have limited useful applications in most street defense situations but would command absolute respect in some home protection situations.

Modern shotguns with a rifled slug barrel are capable of putting a projectile weighing 1 ounce or more into a 2" to 3" group at 100 yards. That's a large piece of lead which is effective on brown bears. The standard 12 gauge 00 buckshot load uses 9 lead balls, each .33 caliber in diameter. This is a common self-defense and police loading for the 12 gauge and it's to be respected by both the shooter, because it kicks hard, and anyone unlucky enough to be in the direction this load is fired.

At the other end of the shotgun spectrum, is the .410 shotgun shell loaded with snake shot fired from a small sized handgun. This load wouldn't seriously injure you if you were wearing a heavy leather coat and were standing at the far end of a long hallway, providing you weren't hit in the face. It won't feel very good, but that load would probably not stop a tough person with bad intentions at longer distances. At close range it will tear one large ragged hole in a man causing death if he were hit in a vulnerable spot. There are other .410 loads fired from a shotgun that are very respectable at more distant home defense ranges.

There's a common misconception among those who have never checked shotgun patterns. Shot patterns left in a large paper target with various shotguns, barrel lengths and loads will be surprising to them. The misconception is that if a bad guy needs to be shot in your home, 'all you have to do is point that 12 gauge in his direction, and you will get him.' I have heard that so many times, it continues to amaze me people think that way.

You MUST at least basically aim that shotgun to be able to hit something if it's any distance at all from you. I can't tell you how far away they have to be before you must aim, instead of just pointing, because I don't know how big your target is, the gauge of your shotgun, the length of your barrel, the type of shot you are using for defense, how good a shot you are and so on. I do know if you are scared because someone is trying to kill you, you shouldn't count on the shotgun doing something magical without you doing your part to hit the target.

Go out and practice at various ranges with various loads. You will learn a shotgun is not magic. You will need to at least point with some degree of accuracy which requires practice if you want to be able to hit something, especially under pressure.

There are serious advantages to using a powerful 00 buck load in a 12 gauge shotgun for home defense. Even the minimum legal length 18" barreled pump shotgun with a legal magazine extension will hold 7 rounds including a loaded chamber. With 9 lead balls in each round a good shotgun shooter can put 63 holes that are .33 caliber each into a target in just a few seconds. This is more good size holes in a target than a full auto submachine gun is capable of delivering in the same amount of time. The usual 30 round magazines that most submachine guns are loaded with can empty fast, but need to be reloaded after 31 shots. What you need all those holes for is usually up for debate, unless there are multiple opponents but the moral of the story is a 12-gauge shotgun is a fearsome weapon.

A police officer working on an Oakland, CA. drug entry team told me when his team made entry, he and another member were both armed with pistol gripped 18 1/2" barreled 12 gauges. One would be fully loaded, round in the chamber, ready to fire if he must.

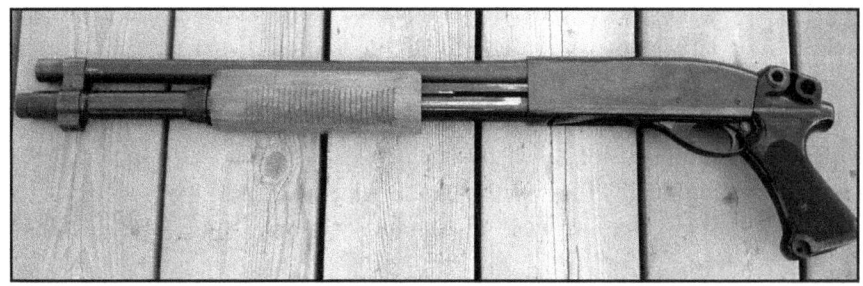
The time tested, battle proven, Remington M870 pump 12 gauge

The other would have an empty chamber and full magazine. After another team member opened the door the guy with the empty chamber would also enter then rack his slide to load his weapon.

Racking the slide creates a distinctive and unmistakable sound of deadly authority, usually commanding instant respect and causing anyone with thoughts of resisting or shooting at the police to stop and give up. Sometimes that didn't work, and the man with the loaded shotgun had to deliver to protect himself or his team members from being shot.

The other side of the story is that, if fired from the shoulder, a 12 gauge loaded with full power 00 buck rounds or slugs will cause a tough person to have a bruised and sore shoulder if they shoot it very many times. Using light practice loads in the 12 gauges makes it much easier to fire more rounds to practice your accuracy. It is necessary to know what full power loads feel like if you want to be prepared for defense.

Being afraid of the shotgun isn't good if you find yourself in trouble. Having practiced and knowing what to expect when you fire it, hopefully means you won't have to fire many rounds. One round of properly placed 00 buckshot usually does the job, and if your life is on the line it's doubtful you will feel recoil.

Short barreled pistol gripped shotguns are usually not recommended for most people because it's harder to hit your target with one. Like anything else, if you are willing to put in the practice, and your wrist doesn't complain too much, you will find the 18" inch barrel very effective at most home defense distances. But you may not. I have run thru shooting stages and courses at the range with my short-barreled shotgun because I like it. I enjoy practicing with the light loads and use some 00 buck loads just to keep me aware of how hard they recoil and smack my hand and wrist. I find merit in using the light loads the trap shooters use to practice quick pointing and shooting accurately from the hip.

A police officer friend from Tucson, AZ. named Darrin aka 'Mongo' and I enjoy going to the range and practicing drills in various made up situations. We time each other as we go through a door set-up at the range, then engage (shoot) 3 targets the other guy has positioned at unknown positions and distances from roughly 3, 5, and 10 yards. Sometimes a 'no shoot' target is up, and sometimes a 'hostage' is placed in front of the bad guy target, leaving very little bad guy to hit.

Besides great fun, these drills keep you mentally and physically sharp. Timing these drills lets you know if you are improving. Knowing you can start on one side of a closed door not knowing where the targets are and, at the go sound, open and go through the door, find and hit all 3 targets with a 12 gauge shotgun in 1.69 seconds gives you confidence with your weapon. Of course safety first is our primary goal and nobody is shooting back at us. We have both practiced with weapons for many years and we know what can happen in a brief instant of carelessness. Most gun ranges will not allow this type of practice by the general public, so be careful!

Due to the punishing recoil of standard 00 buck, some police departments use 12 gauge 00 buck light load rounds which many officers appreciate. These 12 gauge light loads are a good alternative to the full power 00 buck loads. Other alternatives for citizens are the 20 gauges, 16 gauges, or even the .410 shotgun. These would also be an option for those small in stature who don't like recoil or maybe have an injury or physical problem which eliminates a 12 gauge for their personal and family defense.

The .410 shotgun is .41 caliber measured in decimal inches but other shotgun gauges are measured by a unique method: A lead ball the diameter of a 12 gauge shotgun bore weighs $1/12^{th}$ of a pound, so it takes 12 lead balls the size of the bore to make a pound. Therefore, a 20 gauge needs 20 lead balls the size of its bore to make a pound and the same for a 16 gauge. This also holds true for the VERY large bores made in England; 4 and 2 gauges. Alan Meyers, in Britain, is making a 1 gauge shotgun large enough to shoot a one-pound ball of lead.

A modern 12 gauge 16 shot double barrel pump shotgun

SPECS	
Model	DP-12
Type	Shotgun
Action	Pump Action
Gauge	12 Ga.
Chamber	2-3/4" & 3"
Barrel Length	18-7/8"
Weight	9 Lbs. 12 oz.
Sights	Picatinny Mounting Rail
Finish: Stock & Forearm	Matte Black Composite
Finish: Barrel & Receiver	Black Steel/Aluminum
Choke	Flush-Mount Spreader/Spreader
Safety	Ambidextrous 2-Position
Capacity	14 + 2

RIFLES

Rifles have been used for self defense for centuries but obviously they are not as useful for most everyday urban street self defense. In rural areas, rifles are found in the rifle rack of many pickup trucks and millions of homes have at least one rifle for home protection.

The effective distance, power and accuracy of the rifle make it a much more desirable fighting weapon than a handgun, if size is not a factor. Clint Smith of Thunder Ranch has said something about "not taking a handgun to a gun fight."

This is a long range rifle in 20x102 mm made by Anzio. For comparison, the .50 BMG round is 12.7x97 mm. With 1,543 gr. solid bullets it has 39,500 ft/pounds of energy at the muzzle, compared to about 14,000 ft/pounds with a typical 750 gr. bullet from the .50 BMG. Andre' Dall'au photo F.W. Demara story, Tactical Weapons magazine

A rifle is better when its size doesn't interfere with its usefulness. An important drawback against using a rifle in a home, is the power factor in many rifles. If you have a home intruder and are forced to shoot him, the bullet can go through the intruder and hurt someone who is innocent. You are also more easily disarmed if you are surprised at close range.

Rifles can be single shot, bolt, lever or pump actions, semi or fully automatic. Rifles can be used from contact distance as a club, out to an effective range of a mile and a half. At that distance one must have a rifle that is obviously above the ordinary and sufficiently powerful to launch a bullet that far.

Rifles can range in power from the .22 short caliber, up to the 20mm military caliber. The .22 short target round with a 29 grain bullet has about 35 ft lbs. of ME (muzzle energy) and the .50 BMG rifle has about 14,000 ft lbs. of ME, with a 750 grain bullet. In comparison, an average 30-06 load using a 180 grain bullet has about 2,900 ft lbs. of ME.

This is the McMillan TAC-50 bolt action sniper rifle in .50 BMG caliber, that set the record for the longest sniper kill. Canadian Forces sniper Rob Furlong, hit an insurgent in Afghanistan, at a laser measured 2,430 meters or 1.51 miles. John Larsen photo/ Andre' M. Dall'au story/ Tactical Weapons magazine

This is a 100 yard, 3 shot group I fired with a M700 Remington in .270 Win using factory 130 gr. Ballistic Silvertip ammo. Group size measures .161 and is slightly enlarged for clarity.

With modern equipment, schooling and practice, one can put a lethal dose of lead poisoning into a very small target from distances that amaze those not familiar with long distance rifle capability. World Record 10 shot groups, fired from 1000 yards, measure less than 2 inches. That's a small sized cluster of bullet holes from 10 football fields, or 120 yards past a half mile. Cartridges firing these groups include the .300 Weatherby Magnum, and .30 WSM.

The smallest group I know of fired from 100 yards, measures .050 inches, using the 6PPC cartridge. These groups are fired by bench rest competitors who are very serious about shooting very small groups from a bench at the rifle range. You don't need to shoot the type of specialized equipment bench rest shooters use for your personal protection and unless there are some very special circumstances, someone so far away is usually not presenting a dangerous threat to you, unless it is some type of war conflict.

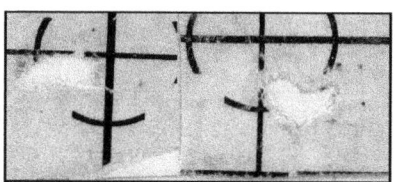

These are the first two, 1 hole, 4 and 3 shot groups I fired from 100 yds about 1983 with my Remington M721 30/06. My rifle shooting coach Tom Price loaded 165 gr. hand loads for me. Both these groups measured sub .2 inch. Once an accurate load is found, the sights are moved to hit the exact mark.

To measure the very small bullet groups, measure from the farthest outside black lines the bullets leave in the target. The bullets usually leave a small black circle on the outside of the bullet hole. After that measurement has been taken with a micrometer, you subtract the diameter of the bullet. For example if a group measures .500, deduct .308 from that if you are shooting a .30 caliber rifle and you have a .192 inch group. This is usually only for measuring groups that all the bullets went into 1 hole.

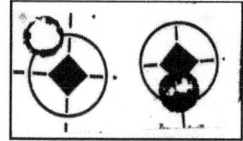

2 shots from 200 yards at 2 dots using .270 Win

Some shooters aren't impressed with that type of shooting because they are hunters or others who know that in real life situations, war or self defense, there's rarely the opportunity to shoot from the optimum accuracy setup, like from the bench at the rifle range.

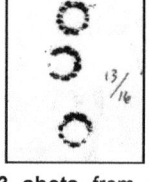

3 shots from **300 yards** with my .270 Win. This group measures 13/16" measured from center to center of the holes. Marine snipers consider this an adequate group to fire from 100 yards

There's much truth and merit to this but on the other hand if a shooter fires one hole groups at the bench, they have confidence in their weapon and cartridge. They know what their equipment is capable of if they do their part. They know with a decent rest to shoot from, hitting someone behind a hostage or only presenting a portion of their head from cover is not difficult if the distance and wind is reasonable.

Short rifles usually chambered for somewhat less powerful cartridges, are called carbines. These are lighter, faster and easier to handle than the average full sized rifle. Carbines are usually but not always, chambered in

For comparison, **L to R** 20x102mm, Anzio 20-50, .50 BMG, 7.62x54R, 7.62 NATO, and the .223. The Anzio 20-50 is a 20mm round necked down to .50 cal. Andre' Dall'au photo, F.W. Demara story, Tactical Weapons magazine.

handgun, or smaller rifle calibers and are sometimes used by police in situations where the distance to the threat is farther than can be effectively engaged with handguns. There is the concern a shotgun blast with buckshot may hit innocents.

The .44 Magnum, .357 Magnum, .45 ACP and 9mm are examples of handgun calibers that have carbines manufactured for them. Carbines have more accuracy, range and power than handguns firing the same cartridge. Longer barrels with iron sights on a carbine give more distance between the front and back sights for more aiming precision than handguns offer. The heavier weight and barrel of a carbine remains steadier and easier to stay on target than a handgun.

Bullets have more velocity when fired from a carbine because pressure from the gases have more time behind the bullet in a longer barrel than the shorter handgun barrel. With additional bullet velocity comes more impact power and a farther effective range than the same cartridge fired from a handgun. It's hard, however, to fit a carbine in your holster.

**There is a NEW WORLD RECORD sniper kill
detailed in the Revised chapter section**

173

THE ATOMIC BULLET

Since the beginning of warfare there has been an effort to deceive the enemy. There are so many examples of ancient as well as modern methods to 'fake out' the enemy an encyclopedia could be written on just that topic.

This is not the place for that and many martial artists really don't care much about how Genghis Khan carried on his conquests. There are; however, many lessons to be learned from this type of history if one is truly interested in the MARTIAL WAY.

I would like to share one example of deception and misinformation just because I found it interesting and humorous. My friend General Bushong shared a story with me that took place during the Korean conflict.

There were spies called 'turncoats' among the South Korean soldiers who were gaining information for the Communists in the North. To psych out these enemy soldiers a plan was formulated to put a dose of fear into the enemy. The plan was to have these 'turncoats' give their leaders some scary news.

A 21 year old 1st Lt. Charles Bushong, is being demonstrated on by Lt. Colonel D'Eliscue during Army Ranger training in Hawaii in 1947. This photo was on the cover on Cosmopolitan Magazine. Retired Brigadier General Bushong served his country in WW II, Korea, and Vietnam, and had many interesting adventures to share. I am very thankful for what he has taught me.

This is **REAL MARTIAL ARTS!**

A meeting place was set up before hand where about 5,000 troops were to be gathered. Up on the side of the mountain near this meeting area a large amount of explosives were hidden and a wire ran down to a location that was going to be out of sight of the assembled soldiers. After everyone was gathered, an American officer showed the assembled troops a spiffed up standard military 30-06 cartridge that, except for being real shiny, was normal in every way.

After a short speech touting the new U.S. secret weapon called the **'Atomic Bullet,'** a rifleman loaded the round into a Garrand battle rifle, aimed at the preselected location where the explosives had been prepared and fired. At that signal the unseen explosive expert triggered the charges and a tremendous explosion rocked the mountain.

It appeared the rifle bullet had caused the big explosion and was a very powerful and dangerous weapon. This of course created quite an impression. It had only been a few years since the Atomic Bombs had been dropped on Japan and that memory was still fresh in many minds.

Acknowledgments

Thank God first. That's what a whole list of Champions in the Spirit chapter have done, so I'm going to keep doing things they have done as I have for so many years. After thanking God, I want to thank my Mother and Father and Helen Kelly Carlin for teaching me how to talk to my God.

In addition to those I have mentioned in the book, I wish to express my gratitude to Mr. Bob Copeland and his sidekick Valerie for providing me with a perfect Writers Haven, Brute 'The Battle Dog' and much more. Irving Anderson, Gary, JR and Grant Jantzer, 'Little Fox' for her Golden Hearted Friendship. Todd Grannis, Larry Hurst, Jim Friend and without 'Dr' Greg Fernandez's technological help, I couldn't have brought this to you. 'IMAX' Doug Memmott, Kevin Clark, 'Killer' Rita Kurz, 'Kamander' Karl Henderson and Scot and Michelle Shearer. Thanks to my brothers Matt and Richard.

Bobbi 'BoSan' McGrath, Lori Cappa, Cassandra 'KO Lady' Phillips, 'Sparky' Bethany Bernbaum, 'Nito' Brandi Wood, Kathy Rowan, Kay Carlson, Jaine Roberston and Mrs Ringo the Amazing Lion and Tiger Trainer. Wayne and Bunny Owens, Bonne Anderson, Lloyd C. 'The Chief' Davis, Darrin 'Mongo' Johnston, Glen Householder and Tony 'The Warrior' McGlothlin. Rob Hisamoto and his git-r-dun assistant Mandy. Larry Derry, Maynard Frank, Ron Maxwell, Clarence and Stuart Baker, Jeff Gill and James E. Dittmer.

Families: The Bud Ballingers, The Mark Timmermans, The Phil and Bret Blackstones, The Gary Blairs, The Jerry Reedys and Karla and Evan Braude. Champion Fighters 'Captain' Chad Staten, Tim 'The Technician' Seig, 'Tiger' Anthony Frye, 'Iron Man' Sean Miller, Nathan 'Monzon' Orchard, Steven 'Grizzly' Keen, and Champion Ernesto 'The Hammer' Duran and Mr. Brady Adams.

Thank you to the following for us to learn martial arts from their Photos:
YouTube, bleacherreport.com, mmanewssource.com, Fox News, Getty Images, bjjee.com, Low Kick MMA, padraigwhelan.wordpress.com, mettachronicle, Luffa-Getty Images, Matt Roberts/USA Today Sports Images, AFP/Getty Images PAUL CROCK, dailymail.co.uk, UFC, ESPN News, The Independent, MMA Fighting, Christian Petersen/Getty Images, EvolutionMMA, chicagonow.com, MMAWiki.org, ufc.com, mma-core.com.

Special thanks to Mr. Leon Rogers at Century Martial Arts Supply, Bob Slack, Gary Jantzer, Vern Collins, The Coey's, Larry Hurst, Bonnie Anderson, Stephan Morris, Kirby Barker.

To my editors: I have too much to thank you for mere words don't measure up. "Angel" Jeri Foutz and her husband 'The Great' Dr. Steven Foutz, 'Pistol' Pete and his 'Eagle Eye' wife Barbara, and Professor Steven Flannery.

With Gratitude and Respect,
James Dolmage

Final Thoughts

I hope you have enjoyed and benefited from the ideas and information presented to you in this book. There were many things I had to leave out due to size restrictions. I did not cover many ways for you to use your body's natural weapons, or how to do many physical techniques for self defense or fighting competitions such as MMA.

As previously mentioned the purpose of this book is to **give your brain the information** it needs to control and train your muscles and body for physical movement and to inspire your spirit. The most enjoyable way to read this work is viewing the full color PDF files on a computer from www.modernmartialarts.com.

There is more info on the website, so feel free to visit there and email your questions, comments or information you deem important. In the Japanese spirit of KAIZEN or 'continual improvement,' I aim to improve, so if you can help me do that, I'll be grateful!

Thanks again,

James Dolmage
jdbudo@msn.com

WHAT IS NEW?

What's new? It has been a handful of years since this book was first written and there have been many new 'happenings' in martial arts during that time. In accordance to the 'modern' in the title of this book, this revision will bring up to date some of the Modern aspects of martial arts.

The information presented earlier has not changed and is absolutely just as pertinent today and will be good for humans in the future.

Traditional martial arts by their very nature have remained mostly unchanged. Thats why they are traditional. MMA has sped up the open-minded approach and there has been an accelerated desire for humans to seek advantages over opponents in a fight. They want to improve themselves because losing in fights hurts or worse or much worse. They want to learn good functional techniques that will help them win regardless of where those moves come from.

MMA has also seemed to bolster those who haven't been taught about the Respect and other virtues that traditional martial arts foster in those who train in those arts.

Many MMA fighters, ESPECIALLY AMATEURS have only been taught the fighting moves and not the character development that traditional martial arts teach. A sizable proportion of these young MMA dudes don't seem to understand that their heroes are using moves that came from traditional martial arts.

A top notch fighter needs to have the natural desire to excel. Staying competitive in todays fiercely competitive MMA fight 'jungle' requires a continual refinement of skills. Where do these fighters that are hungry for skills, knowledge and technical fighting skills go? These fighters go to learn from forward thinkers that have learned traditional martial arts but have recognized the value of open minded training.

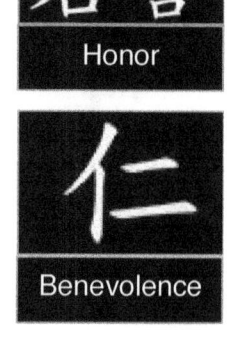

There are so many reasons and benefits to regular practice of the different martial arts. Not everyone trains for the same reasons. Everyone that pursues martial arts does so for their own individual reasons. If an individual is not training in the Earths Most Deadly Art and they know it and thats OK with them, then so be it. They may not care anything about that. They may enjoy what they are doing and are happy with the benefits they getting, whatever those benefits are.

Loyalty

The problem is when they think they are a badass but they are mostly just mislead. There are many videos on YouTube showing martial arts fraud and shear folly. There are practitioners who think all is well but it isn't.

Rectitude

There are also a share of folks who are totally into their style of martial arts whatever it may be and actually believe they have knowledge, skills and ability. This is a sad thing when I see real young kids or unskilled, unfit, overweight people taking black belt tests. For the life of me I can't understand how a 'Special Certificate' of any kind is going to give someone abilities they really don't have. It used to be a black belt was a bad ass. That is no longer always the case.

Chloe Bruce Scorpion Kick Tutorial   YouTube

On the other hand there are some amazing athletes that do things today that nobody could do in the past. If Chloe Bruce wasn't so good looking I would think she is an alien from space.

I have tried to be a good student during the 51 years I have been training and I am very grateful to all who have taught me. Perhaps the two biggest changes I have seen this past half century training is the number of people in martial arts who are more 'open-minded' regarding learning from other martial arts 'styles' and overweight people especially 'Master' or 'Grandmasters.'

If it's a student that is too heavy, then good for them they are there improving their health and fitness. An instructor especially a high ranking black belt should not be fat and out of shape unless they have a serious medical issue.

A big fat person regardless of belt rank or certificate is still a big fat person who is not healthy and doesn't represent true health and fitness offered with Martial Arts training. I am not your dad or the boss of you. I am also not the boss of martial arts. My friend Mr. Kirby Barker uses JMO (just my opinion) and I like that, so all of the things I write are JMO even if it offends some people.

 Centers for Disease Control and Prevention
CDC 24/7: Saving Lives, Protecting People™

According to the **National** Institutes of Health, **obesity** and overweight together are the second leading cause of preventable **death** in the **United States**, close behind tobacco use (3). An estimated 300,000 **deaths** per year are due to the **obesity** epidemic (57).

 World Health Organization

Obesity and overweight
Fact sheet
Updated June 2016

Key facts

- Worldwide obesity has more than doubled since 1980.
- In 2014, more than 1.9 billion adults, 18 years and older, were overweight. Of these over 600 million were obese.
- 39% of adults aged 18 years and over were overweight in 2014, and 13% were obese.
- Most of the world's population live in countries where overweight and obesity kills more people than underweight.
- 41 million children under the age of 5 were overweight or obese in 2014.
- Obesity is preventable.

Obesity is common, serious and costly

- More than one-third (36.5%) of U.S. adults have obesity. [Read CDC National Center for Health Statistics (NCHS) data brief   (https://www.cdc.gov/nchs/data/databriefs/db219.pdf) PDF-704KB]
- Obesity-related conditions include heart disease, stroke, type 2 diabetes and certain types of cancer, some of the leading causes of preventable death. [Read guidelines (http://www.nhlbi.nih.gov/health-pro/guidelines/archive/clinical-guidelines-obesity-adults-evidence-report)   ]
- The estimated annual medical cost of obesity in the U.S. was $147 billion in 2008 U.S. dollars; the medical costs for people who are obese were $1,429 higher than those of normal weight. [Read summary (http://content.healthaffairs.org/cgi/reprint/28/5/w822)   ]

Obesity affects some groups more than others

[Read abstract *Journal of American Medicine (JAMA)* (http://jama.jamanetwork.com/article.aspx?articleid=1832542)   ]

- Non-Hispanic blacks have the highest age-adjusted rates of obesity (48.1%) followed by Hispanics (42.5%), non-Hispanic whites (34.5%), and non-Hispanic Asians (11.7%). Obesity is higher among middle age adults age 40-59 years (40.2%) and older adults age 60 and over (37.0%) than among younger adults age 20–39 (32.3%).

Newer Fighters

The following observations are absolutely not meant to pick on individual fighters. I am just using them as current examples to illustrate how different types of training affects a fighters capabilities in general.

Newer fighters that have created a buzz in the mixed martial arts world include MMA fighters Connor McGregor, Rhonda Rousey, Holly Holm, Jon Jones, Steven 'Wonder Boy' Thompson and of course many more.

Except for WB (Wonder Boy) all of these fighters have been a UFC Champion and excelled in one way or another. WB fought to a draw with Champion Tyrone Woodley according to the judges recently but I thought Wonder Boy won the fight.

Successful MMA fighters are continually evolving. They learn and practice more technically complicated fighting skills and put them to use in recent fights. Just a few years ago the idea of watching a former Heavyweight UFC Champ run across the Octagon, jump and deliver a flying side kick to the face of a 6'7" opponent in the Octagon would be somewhat laughable. The kick hurt Browne but didn't land quite right for the KO. Today even heavyweights are knocking out opponents with spin kicks to the head.

A great example of advanced technical striking skill is watching the proficiency of Wonder Boy while he dismantled former UFC 170 lb. Champ Johny Hendricks. This fight was very satisfying to watch from a technicians perspective.

WB used his lead leg side kick to the body and hook kick to Hendricks face. WB baffled and easily picked Hendricks apart with confusing kick-punch combinations that he had not trained to see, recognize and respond appropriately to. Hendricks had zero good answers for Wonder Boys skills.

Former UFC World Heavyweight Champ Fabricio Werdum delivers flying side kick to Travis Browne.
YouTube

Former Heavyweight UFC Champ knocks out Mark Hunt with spin kick to the head.　　bleacherreport.com

Browne vs Mitrione
mmanewsource.com

This is not pick on Johny Hendricks day I like him. I can relate to the wrestler in him training for strength, endurance and standard basic kickboxing techniques. Then suddenly having to deal with quicker, more confusing, karate free style point fighting movement mixed in with solid punches.

In high school, Hendricks was a 3 time Oklahoma State Wrestling Champ and a 2 time National Wrestling Champ. In college he was a NCAA National Champion and a 4 time All-American wrestler. Johny is tough!

Twice before this fight, and later at UFC 207, Hendricks missed making weight. He had conditioning issues, so to prepare for WB he worked real hard on strength and conditioning. Johny stated before the WB fight how 'ready' he was and how great of 'condition' he was in.

It was true! Johny looked great and had strength, cardio and endurance conditioning for more of a grappling type contest or football game, but not a **fight** with someone who practiced a lot of takedown defense and who possessed superior striking skills.

Hendricks had been doing 'Hamster' training, which again is simple training like the hamster running around on the wheel which is very good for the hamster but the actual movements won't end a fight.

The best way to see and really understand about current **fight** training methods and how those different methods affects your body, would be to watch *'Johny Hendricks Strength and Conditioning Training Muscle Madness 1'* on YouTube. He works really hard to prepare for Fight Night 82 against WB.

Then watch *'UFC Fight night 82 Stephen Thompson workout highlights'* on YouTube. After comparing vastly different training methods, watch these 2 men fight on YouTube. See what happens to the **strongest** man, and what happens to the man who practices **Avoiding and Delivering Power.** Fun contest! The stronger more 'conditioned' man gets brutalized. The technically superior man goes home happy as an unmarked winner.

Hendricks vs Thompson Fox News

Thompson lead leg hook kick to Hendricks. Getty images

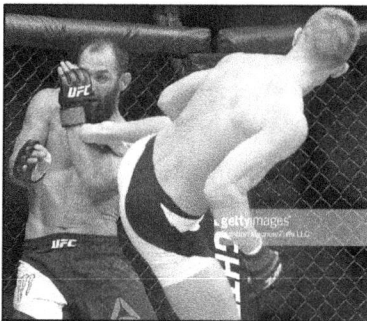

Thompson turning sidekick. Getty Images

Sharp accurate punches. bjjee.com

My website includes numerous video examples of men, some LITERALLY TWICE their opponents size getting absolutely schooled by smaller, 'weaker' but *more technically trained* men and women. Links to these videos can be found in the Sample Chapter - Strength Training tab. Every martial artist should view these examples to appreciate the benefits martial arts training has for people who want to improve themselves.

Thompson vs Woodley
Low Kick MMA

Another recent example of technical fighting is when Wonder Boy fought the 170 lb. UFC Champ Tyrone Woodley. As previously mentioned the judges called the WB vs Woodley fight a draw but in my opinion WB won.At the post fight interview Woodley, who was also a extremely powerful wrestler, stated that to prepare for the WB fight he had karate type sparring partners throwing countless kicks at him. That karate type preparation saved Woodley from a similar fate that Hendricks met.

While on the WB vs Woodley fight I wanted to state my opinion. In the 4th round of their fight, Woodley caught WB and knocked him down, did some ground and pound and caught WB in a deep guillotine choke. WB toughed it out and ended the round on top beating on Woodley. One judge scored that round a 10-8 round for Woodley. As a fighter I sometimes wonder at the wisdom of having people who have never fought before, judge fights.

Silva vs Sonnen
padraigwhelan.wordpress.com

To me it looked like a rough 4th round for sure for WB, but sometimes I don't believe non fighters understand that just because it LOOKS like a fighter is getting hurt, it doesn't mean he is getting hurt as bad as the judge thinks. Too me if fighter A is seemingly getting thrashed for most of the round but survives and turns the tables

Sonnen in the Trap.
mettachronicle

on fighter B at the end of the round, then I give high marks for effective defensive skills, surviving and turning the tables. Apparently WB wasn't hurt as bad as many thought or he wouldn't have wound up on top pounding Woodley at the end of the round.

Anderson Silva wanted to stay on his feet but sometimes he would get taken down. When that happened, Silva would stay relaxed and it looked as if he is getting enthusiastically ground and pounded real good by his opponent like Chael Sonnen on top. In reality what he was doing was the same thing Muhammed Ali would do by laying on the ropes and letting his opponent wear himself out.

I enjoyed watching Master Silva drain his opponents strength from the bottom position. Since he is on the bottom and it appears he is getting beaten up, he must be getting hurt and beat up. Unless one has been a fighter its more difficult to understand that it really doesn't matter what it looks like unless it goes to a decision with the judges.

Holm making Rousey miss and making her pay.
Zuffa-Getty Images

It really only matters if the person on the bottom is actually really getting hurt, NOT what appears to be happening to the less informed. This is important to know as a fighter, as is being aware of how much energy your opponent is expending and taking advantage of them if they have put on a energy draining burst especially late in a round or fight.

The names Ronda Rousey and Connor McGregor may be the most famous current MMA fighters. Ronda found out that judo and boxing skills are not enough to get past Holly Holm who is a much more technically skilled opponent who mixes up excellent take down defense with confusing kick-punch combinations. It was quite a surprise to the grappler/jiujitsu fans who were certain nobody could withstand Rousey's furious takedown attacks.

Holm 'man handling' Rousey.
Matt Roberts/USA Today Sports Images

As long as MMA stands for mixed MARTIAL ARTS then there should be Champions who represents the martial arts the way they should be represented. In my opinion Holly Holm is a VASTLY better representation of the Virtues that martial arts teach. Ronda Rouseys' foul mouth, bird flipping finger and general Miss Bad Ass attitude are not the way that martial arts masters teach students to behave.

Holm fight ending roundhouse kick to Rousey.
AFP/Getty Images PAUL CROCK

In her defense the UFC encourages drama. Listening to Rousey state she could whip men like former UFC heavyweight champion Cain Velasquez or Floyd Mayweather made me have a tendency to forget her greatness as a grappler.

McGregor takes out Mendes.
dailymail.co.uk

Holly Holm in turn went out fighting a choke and lost consciousness to Meisha Tate. She also lost a decision to Valentia Shevchenko. To me Holly was too predictable and lacked surprise by using just basic kickboxing techniques. Shevchenko has been doing martial arts for many more years than Holly. Because of that varied experience Shevchenko was able to recognize Holly's' movement and counter her.

Connor McGregor has showed he really is a fighter and will fight anywhere between 145-170 lbs. There are many things I enjoy about watching him fight but I wish he would not talk like he is at a bar after he beats up his opponents. Once again I don't believe young people need to watch Champions talk and act like regular disrespectful assholes influencing youth to then act the way the Champ does. He is the leading money maker in the UFC for 2016.

After the fight, I learned an interesting thing about McGregor fighting 2 time NCAA All-American Wrestler Chad Mendes. McGregor's coach stated that due to a recovering knee injury, McGregor had done NO WRESTLING in preparation for fighting a wrestler.

Actual wrestling practice isn't really needed if you already have decent grappling skills, know and understand basic submissions and defenses and you train hard to prevent being taken down. Of course you need to develop superior striking skills that grapplers can't deal with. I found that admission by McGregor's coach to be very satisfying and showed I was 100% correct in my training wrestlers to leave that training alone and go start kicking.

The distance that a good *effective kicker* commands makes takedowns very very difficult. The Man who owns the **most UFC records** attempted a remarkable **4 Take Downs in his UFC career. Thats a FACT.**

As previously stated, the faster the wrestler shoots in to cover that distance, the worse it hurts when a well timed, accurate punch lands. That extra distance a kicker controls gives a defender just a bit of extra time to counter the attempt and the incoming energy is technically place on the attackers vulnerable spot.

McGregor's fight ending one punch to Jose Aldo's jaw as Aldo rushed in eager to smash McGregor is as fine an example of Bruce Lee's - Speed, Timing, Accuracy equals Power, as can be viewed and learned from.

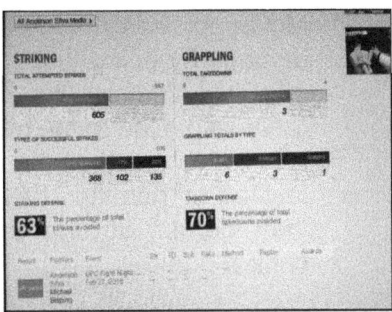

Anderson Silva holds **UFC** records for **Most Wins, Consecutive Title Defenses, Most Knock Downs**, **Longest Win Streak** 2,457 days. #2 in **KO's** and #3 in **Post Fight Bonuses.** UFC

Vitor Belfort owns the **UFC record** for **Most KO's.** Silva maintains distance and KO's him with effective traditional kick.
ESPN News

McGregor 1 punch to Aldo.
The Independant

McGregor has the ability to judge distance and avoid damage by being just out of range but be close enough to effectively deliver his counter techniques. His timing is great also. One of the most important reasons he has those abilities is the **time** he spends doing sparring type drills. Instead of 'hamster' training, McGregor gets a partner and they deliver striking techniques back and forth under control.

Another eye poke from Jones.   MMA Fighting

They spend extra **time** *delivering* techniques and combinations and *watching* techniques and combinations come toward them under control slowly at first, then up to full speed. They use the proper defenses for those incoming techniques, over and over and over, which gives him abilities. Those abilities can't be matched by fighters who are looking in the mirror lifting weight, running, grappling or 'doing cardio.' You get real good at delivering and defending against power.

Rousey again learned the hard way that **Avoiding and Delivering Power** practice works best in a *fight*.
Christian Petersen/Getty Images

Those types of drills are what fighters practice if they want to 'see' faster, react more effectively and have the correct distance. That kind of movement is what will happen in a fight, so this is what he spends a lot of **time** doing. That type of training has paid off very well for Wonder Boy, Silva, and McGregor! Another thing that has improved lately for many MMA fighters especially in the UFC is more money they are making now than in the past.

The top fighters don't make money like other top performers in pro sports yet but things are moving along better for them in that regard. Rousey just made $3 Million for receiving a 48 second face smashing by Nunes in UFC 207 at the close of 2016. According to a website McGregor made nearly $8 Million in 2016.

Jon Jones has had many troubles outside of the Octagon and he hasn't fought as much as he could have. Jones has great natural talent and abilities as a fighter. One thing I have observed from Jones is he enjoys whipping someone at their own game instead of using his reach and standing technical superiority to end fights sooner.

I believe at times Jones has taken more abuse than he needed to just to really prove a point to his opponent, to himself, or the crowd. I also think he should quit kicking opponents knees, there are enough knee injuries as it is and he should stop poking opponents in the eyes with his fingers. I wish the UFC would enforce strict rules about both those targets. There are many more deserving MMA fighters who could be written about but the main idea here is a person that practices martial arts technical skills will usually defeat a larger stronger person who relies more on size and strength. It is much more fun to win with proper training!

Penetration Test

This is a military bullet penetration test to learn the true capabilities of this type of military round. These photos aid the description of the construction of AP (armor piercing) bullets

This is a 1" thick block of iron shot with AP ammo from my 30/06 over 30 years ago. I enjoy experimenting to find out just what this former military caliber is capable of. Two AP rounds punched right thru the iron and one AP round got stuck. As previously described the AP bullet has a steel or other extremely hard alloy core for weight, with a copper jacket that prevents steel against steel friction as the bullet travels out the barrel.

The front side shows the copper jackets the core has shed while passing right thru. The other bullet core didn't make it all the way thru and the bullet base can be seen. If loaded with AP ammo this is the steel core a old .30 caliber M1 Garrand rifle fired in WWII, Korea and more.

The 2 smooth craters are 180 gr. Remington Core-Lokt hunting bullets made for deep penetration before expansion. The FMJ (full metal jacket) has a lead, or newer ammo uses a non toxic core for weight, then a steel jacket for increased penetration and a copper jacket over that for friction prevention.

It seems we would be safe using a 1" thick iron barrier for cover but apparently with full size battle rifles shooting AP rounds, perhaps not. Remember *concealment* hides you but wont stop bullets and *cover* will stop bullets.

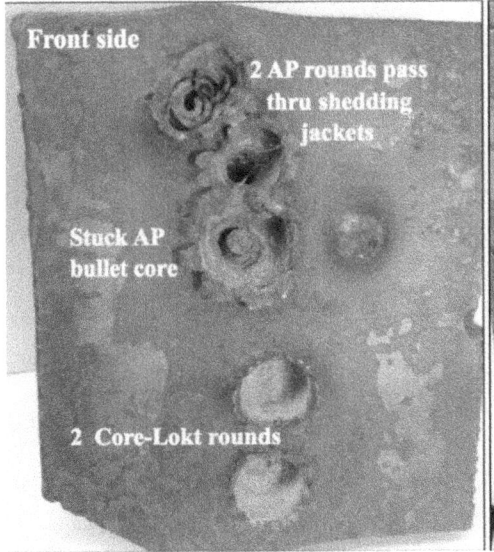
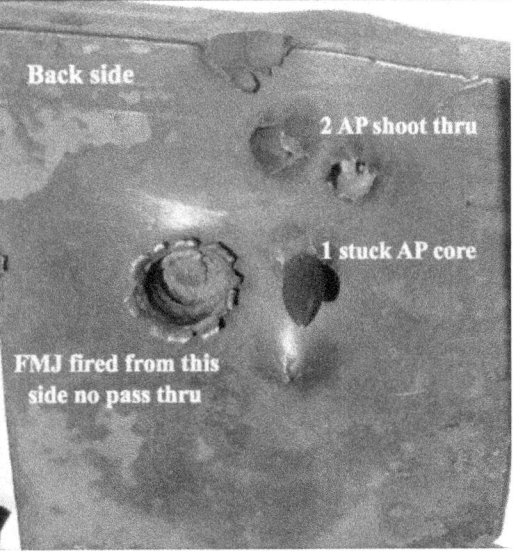

Close up of steel core core after a 1" trip thru iron.

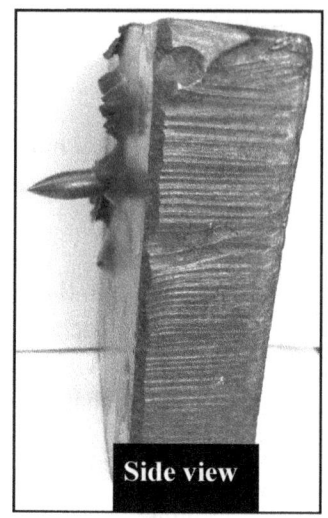
Side view

The 30/06 cartridge has been used in the U.S. for 110 years and is widely available. This is far from the most powerful cartridge available but the bullets it shoots are respected. As previously mentioned todays military .223 is a *scaled down* 30/06 and the .50 BMG is a *scaled up* 30/06.

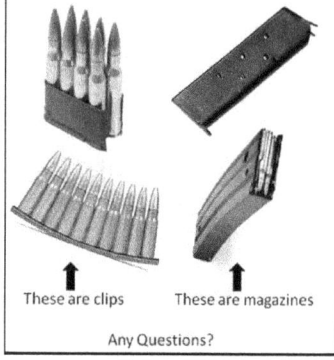
These are clips   These are magazines
Any Questions?

This is certainly not life and death information but there is a continued misuse of these firearms terms. If you use the correct terminology firearms people have more respect for your knowledge ;-)

Above are the primary rifle cartridges used by the U.S. Military since 1906.
L to R
.223 (5.56 x 45 mm)
.308 (7.62 x 51 mm)
30/06 (7.62 x 63 mm)
.50 BMG (12.7 x 99 mm)

NEW WORLD RECORD SNIPER KILL

1. Corporal of Horse (CoH) Craig Harrison, Household Cavalry (UK)
Distance: 2,707 yd
Date: November 2009
Firearm: Accuracy International L115A3
Ammunition: .338 Lapua Magnum LockBase B408 bullets
Conflict: War in Afghanistan

2,707 yards = 2,475 meters

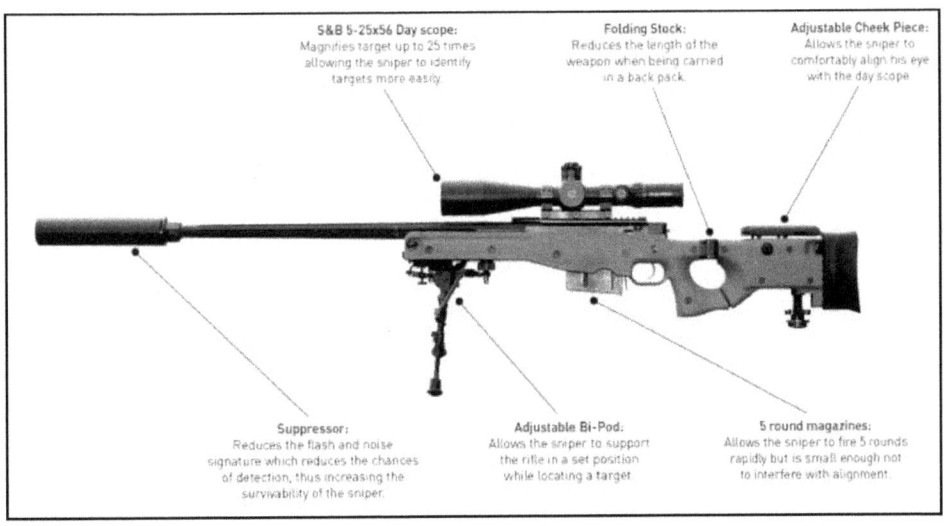

S&B 5-25x56 Day scope: Magnifies target up to 25 times allowing the sniper to identify targets more easily.

Folding Stock: Reduces the length of the weapon when being carried in a back pack.

Adjustable Cheek Piece: Allows the sniper to comfortably align his eye with the day scope.

Suppressor: Reduces the flash and noise signature which reduces the chances of detection, thus increasing the survivability of the sniper.

Adjustable Bi-Pod: Allows the sniper to support the rifle in a set position while locating a target.

5 round magazines: Allows the sniper to fire 5 rounds rapidly but is small enough not to interfere with alignment.

www.ingramcontent.com/pod-product-compliance
Lightning Source LLC
Chambersburg PA
CBHW081231170426
43198CB00017B/2719